NOTHING BUT THE BLOOD

ALEXANDER J FISCHER

Copyright © 2026 by Alexander J Fischer

All rights reserved.

No part of this book may be reproduced in any form or by any electronic or mechanical means, including information storage and retrieval systems, without written permission from the author, except for the use of brief quotations in a book review.

For God, the Son, and the Holy Spirit

1

1: WHAT'S THIS ABOUT BLOOD?

Perhaps you've heard mention of the saying, "You need to get right with God". Maybe you have no clue what that saying even means. Perhaps someone said, "You need Jesus." It might've sparked indignation, confusion, or outright anger. I don't know you, your heart, or your identity. Frankly, I don't need to. We're going to start strong and tell you exactly what you need to understand. Afterward, we'll dip into expounding with scripture and hopefully bring encouragement for the weary as we await our blessed hope.

Let's start with the often-repeated chastisement we've all likely heard or read thrust in our direction. Let's examine the phrase "You need to get right with God".

What's getting right with God even mean? Does it mean "repenting of sins to go to heaven"? See, so many of us either believed or currently believe just this. After all, popular media has belabored this point in many cartoons or movies, hasn't it? Oh, this evil character's done some heinous things, so they're obviously going to hell, right?

Or maybe the heroic main character does some miraculous act of self-sacrifice, and they go to heaven? We're all familiar with these tropes in media of all forms, ranging from video games to television, movies, novels, and beyond. Heck, I'm guilty of this in my own fictional novels. It makes for fun entertainment, but we're not here for entertainment, are we? We're here for our eternal fates.

Our baser human instincts tell us that justice must be served. That the good go to heaven and the bad to hell. Am I wrong? It makes logical sense, and deep down we want to see wicked members of society "get theirs", right? After all, if you've ever been evangelized to, maybe the believer told you that God is a righteous God.

He is righteous, for the record. Now, getting right with God's simple to explain, and yet so many mess it up. It's so simple even a child can understand, and yet 'educated' scholars grapple with the concept. We humans love to over-complicate things and mess them up if you haven't noticed.

Want to get right with God? Here's how.

In 1st Corinthians 15:1-4. "Moreover, brethren, I declare unto you the gospel which I preached unto you, which also ye have received, and wherein ye stand; By which also ye are saved, if ye keep in memory what I preached unto you, unless ye have believed in vain. For I delivered unto you first of all that which I also received, how that Christ died for our sins according to the scriptures; And that he was buried, and that he rose again the third day according to the scriptures."

The old-style English from the King James Version of the Bible can be a little challenging to decipher, so let's delve deeper into those verses, shall we? After all, they're important to our eternal destinies.

It essentially means that you must know Christ died on the cross. Notice it said, "How that Christ died for our sins according to the scriptures." Folks miss that one paltry word: "how". Why is the "how" important? Simple. The blood of Jesus is what washes away our sins.

Maybe you're aware of sin, maybe you're not. What you need to know is you've sinned, same as me, your mom, and mine too. Everyone has - minus Jesus of course. Here's proof in Romans 3:9-12: "What then? are we better than they? No, in no wise: for we have before proved both Jews and Gentiles, that they are all under sin; As it is written, There is none righteous, no, not one: There is none that understandeth, there is none that seeketh after God. They are all gone out of the way, they are together become unprofitable; there is none that doeth good, no, not one." As additional food for thought, here's Romans 3:23-26: "For all have sinned, and come short of the glory of God; Being justified freely by his grace through the redemption that is in Christ Jesus: Whom God hath set forth to be a propitiation through faith in his blood, to declare his righteousness for the remission of sins that are past, through the forbearance of God; To declare, I say, at this time his righteousness: that he might be just, and the justifier of him which believeth in Jesus."

Think of sin as a debt because we broke God's laws. Now we must pay this debt, right? Well, the problem is the only way we can personally pay is by being separated from God for all eternity. This is, to put it mildly, undesirable for everyone involved. We don't want to burn in hell, and neither does the good Lord want us there.

Here's the good news, the best news of all time, I'd wager. Jesus died on the cross to pay for our sins. You might ask, "How's that erase my sin debt? A little blood and that's it?"

Yes, and no. It's a long explanation, but the shortened version is this. It's not the blood of animals like cattle or goats like in the Old Testament that washes us clean. There was an offering made approximately 2000 years ago on your behalf. In fact, Christ's sacrifice and finished work on the cross is payment for all mankind's sins. He lived a sinless life and was the perfect sacrifice for the atonement of our sins. His perfect blood is the only thing that washes us clean in God's eyes.

When folks say, "There's power in the blood", this is what they mean. Jesus' sacrificial blood atonement paid for humanity's sins. All we need to do is believe it and know that he resurrected on the third day, according to the scriptures.

In the Old Testament, the Jewish people sacrificed annually for the entirety of Israel's sins, but that's all done now. As Christ said on the cross, "It is finished." He wasn't talking about his mortal life on Earth. He was referring to the sin problem of mankind.

The only requirement of you, me, and everyone else is to believe that Christ's blood and his sacrifice washes us clean of our iniquities and sins. You trust his blood payment, death, sacrifice, and understand that he resurrected on the third day. In God's eyes, we're righteous afterward.

"That's it?"

Yes, that is the gospel of salvation for all. Some love to overcomplicate it and add or subtract, but that's a whole different mistake.

Note that it isn't "just" Christ's death that saves. "HOW that Christ died." He didn't die of a heart attack, or heatstroke, or drowning, but from willingly bleeding out on a cross for our sakes. The blood washes us clean. His perfect blood and sacrifice was the ultimate atonement for our sins - past, present, and future. Know that the Father raised the Son on the third day. You believe those facts, you're saved.

Done, period. No ifs, ands, or buts to be found in scripture anywhere. Put that proverbial worry on the shelf. Don't take my word for it. Take God's. The most quoted verse in the Bible: John 3:16-18 — says "For God so loved the world, that he gave his only begotten Son, that whosoever believeth in him should not perish, but have everlasting life. For God sent not his Son into the world to condemn the world; but that the world through him might be saved. He that believeth on him is not condemned: but he that believeth not is condemned already, because he hath not believed in the name of the only begotten Son of God."

Want more assurance? Sure. The Bible's full of it. Here's John 10:27-30. This is Jesus speaking, to be clear. "My sheep hear my voice, and I know them, and they follow me: And I give unto them eternal life; and they shall never perish, nether shall any man pluck them out of my hand. My father, which gave them me, is greater than all; and no man is able to pluck them out of my Father's hand. I and my Father are one."

You want more? Sure, here you go. Romans 10:9: "That if thou shalt confess with thy mouth the Lord Jesus, and shalt believe in thine heart that God hath raised him from the dead, thou shalt be saved."

Since we're on a roll, let's keep it going. In Acts 16:25-34, it says this. In this Paul and Silas are imprisoned and their jailor asks how to be saved. "And at midnight Paul and Silas prayed, and sang praises unto God: and the prisoners heard them. And suddenly there was a great earthquake, so that the foundations of the prison were shaken: And immediately all the doors were opened, and everyone's bands were loosed. And the keeper of the prison awakening out of his sleep, and seeing the prison doors open, he drew out his sword, and would have killed himself, supposing that the prisoners had fled. But Paul cried with a loud voice, saying, Do thyself no harm: for we are all here. Then he called for a light, and sprang in, and came trembling, and fell down before Paul and Silas, And brought them out, and said Sirs, what must I do to be saved? And they said, Believe on the Lord Jesus Christ, and thou shalt be saved, and thy house. And they spake unto him the word of the Lord, and to all that were in his house. And he took them the same hour of the night, and washed their stripes; and was baptized, he and all his, straightway. And when he had brought them into his house, he set meat before them, and rejoiced, believing in God with all his house."

Assuming you believe in Christ's atoning blood payment for your sin, you're going in the rapture. You're going to be with the Lord if you die, and you know with 100% certainty. The proof you believe is that you believe it. Simple, isn't it? There's no "standards for holy behavior" or whatever heresy people spew out. If only the righteous went to heaven, then Jesus, God, his Holy Spirit and few others would be there. Perhaps unborn children that God doesn't impute sin to would be there besides. God wants everyone to believe on His Son as evidenced by John 6:39-40. This is Jesus speaking. "And this is the Father's will which hath sent me, that of all which he hath given me I should lose nothing, but should raise it up again at the last day. And this is the will of Him that sent me, that every one which seeth the Son, and believeth on him, may have everlasting life: and I will raise him up at the last day."

Did He say, "conditional life"? No. How about, "If you act obedient, you receive everlasting life?" No? Huh, I guess He meant if you believe, you have eternal life. Take him at his word, folks. Don't overcomplicate it, for your own sake.

In fact, once we're saved through our belief, the Bible

says this in Galatians 4:4-7: "But when the fulness of the time was come, God sent forth his Son, made of a woman, made under the law, To redeem them that were under the law, that we might receive the adoption of sons. And because ye are sons, God hath sent forth the Spirit of his Son into your hearts, crying, Abba, Father. Wherefore thou art no more a servant, but a son; and if a son, then an heir of God through Christ."

Once we believe, we are no longer servants. Isn't that wondrous news? We're heirs of God, aka sons and daughters.

Remember this important fact, folks, when unbelievers try to lead you astray. You might have heard, "I refuse to believe in a God who sends people to hell."

God doesn't really send people to hell. Those people send themselves there. God has given us an out, a readily available gift to avoid hell. It's up to us whether we receive it by believing him or not. If you refuse to believe, you're basically saying, "Nah, I'll pay my debt myself." Then you're sending yourself to the lake of fire.

Now, you may have heard other claims about the way to heaven. We'll go over the false gospels in a later chapter, but I don't want you to think about them now. Focus entirely on the bloodstained gospel, for it is the correct and only true one.

Think of it this way. Maybe you have a child. If not, you surely have/had a mother and father. If your dear loved one got in real trouble, would you sacrifice yourself to save their life?

Most parents, brothers, sisters, children, etc. would say yes. After all, you love them. You don't want them hurt, right? Well, God's perfect in all ways, including love. Why would he choose differently? There's a reason we call him our heavenly Father in the Lord's Prayer. He'd have us call Him Father, and we're beyond blessed to be His children.

So basically, believe Jesus died on the cross after He lived a sinless life. He did this to pay the blood atonement for the world's collective sins — past, present, and future. Know that He died on the cross, was buried, and rose on the third day as scripture says. That's it. That's what "Getting right with God" means.

It's so simple that even a child can understand it. You're not righteous because of anything you do down here on Earth. You cannot add even a drop of anything else to the gospel of salvation. Just understand the simplicity and trust God's word on the subject. He is perfect, all-knowing, and loves us all more than we can imagine.

If needed, take a break, pray to our Father. This book will still be here.

2

2: OUR BLESSED HOPE

A main reason you might've heard to "get right with God" is because of this doctrine called "The Rapture". Some say it's unbiblical. These people likely don't read their Bibles, because it's pretty darn clear. There's a perfect reason that Jesus is called our blessed hope. There are multiple reasons for calling Him such.

The chief reason is because without His sacrifice, we would be condemned to the lake of fire after the first sin of our life. Remember, the wages of sin is death as said in Romans 6:23: "For the wages of sin is death; but the gift of God is eternal life through Jesus Christ our Lord."

That's a monumental reason in its own right. The second is the more widespread idea.

The second reason is an even more controversial doctrine in modern times. Why? I've no clue beyond the enemy trying to steal people's joy and hope. That old serpent, Satan, loves to steal us born-again believers' joy and assurance of salvation at every turn. Why? It's the only trick he has against us - and folks, the devil hates us.

Lots of believers become deceived and deceive others in

turn. I'm of the opinion that this explains the nonsensical hatred that the rapture doctrine receives in modern times.

I imagine you're asking, "But, Alexander, what is this rapture you're talking about? Is this that 'Darby' thing people crow on about? Didn't he come up with this fanciful rapture stuff?"

That's a solid question, and I'm happy you're curious to learn more about our blessed hope. Now, I'm not a Bible scholar, admittedly, but I can at least explain the basics as I understand them. No, Darby was NOT the one who 'came up' with the rapture. The Bible references it several times, as you're about to read.

Many rapture deniers love spouting the same thing. They say, "The word rapture isn't in the Bible. Checkmate, rapture escapists."

The word rapture, in fact, isn't; but to claim the rapture event isn't described is outright wrong. In fact, many verses describe just that with the words "caught up" or "receive you unto myself."

Here's a primary "rapture" verse the Bible contains. It's 1st Thessalonians 4:13-18: "But I would not have you to be ignorant, brethren, concerning them which are asleep, that ye sorrow not, even as others which have no hope. For if we believe that Jesus died and rose again, even so them also which sleep in Jesus will God bring with him. For this we say unto you by the word of the Lord, that we which are alive and remain unto the coming of the Lord shall not prevent them which are asleep. For the Lord himself shall descend from heaven with a shout, with the voice of the archangel, and with the trump of God: and the dead in Christ shall rise first: Then we which are alive and remain shall be **caught up** together with them in the clouds, to meet the Lord in the air: and so shall we ever be with the Lord. Wherefore comfort one another with these words."

Note how it mentions we meet the Lord 'in the air'? It does not say his foot touches down on the Mount of Olives. That proves to me that this is not when Jesus returns with his armies in tow. His armies include us, I believe. So how then could we return with him if we're still down here? It's simple; we're called up before these next verses happen. Look at Zechariah 14:1-5: "Behold, the day of the LORD cometh, and thy spoil shall be divided in the midst of thee. For I will gather all nations against Jerusalem to battle; and the city shall be taken, and the houses rifled, and the women ravished; and half of the city shall go forth into captivity, and the residue of the people shall not be cut off from the city. Then shall the LORD go forth, and fight against those nations, as when he fought in the day of battle. And his feet shall stand in that day upon the mount of Olives, which is before Jerusalem on the east, and the mount of Olives shall cleave in the midst thereof toward the east and toward the west, and there shall be a very great valley; and half of the mountain shall remove toward the north, and half of it toward the south. And ye shall flee to the valley of the mountains; for the valley of the mountains shall reach unto Azal: yea, ye shall flee, like as ye fled from before the earthquake in the days of Uzziah king of Judah: and the LORD my God shall come, and all the saints with thee."

How in the world would we (the saints) return with the Lord like Zechariah says if we don't go up beforehand? We (born again believers) are the saints referenced just earlier, for goodness' sake! Also, don't those two examples (Returning in the air, and his return on the Mount of Olives) seem completely different? One's a joyous occasion, and the other's of judgement.

Now, many, including myself, believe 1st Thessalonians 4:13-18 is referring to the rapture event. One reason is that the Greek translation originally wasn't "caught up," but harpazo. Harpazo in the Greek language is more accurately translated as "snatching away out of danger." Here's another verse that you may remember. I quote this often myself because it's so encouraging. It's John 14:1-3: "Let not your heart be troubled: ye believe in God, believe also in me. In my Father's house are many mansions: if it were not so, I would have told you. I go to prepare a place for you. And if I go and prepare a place for you, I will come again, and receive you unto myself; that where I am, there ye may be also."

Now, let us continue that verse and hear one of the most important quotes of Jesus in the entire Bible. John 14:4 - 6: "And whither I go ye know, and the way ye know. Thomas saith unto him, Lord, we know not whither thou goest; and how can we know the way? Jesus saith unto him, I am the way, the truth, and the life: no man cometh unto the Father, but by me."

Now, let's connect this verse with another and let scripture interpret scripture, which is the best way to interpret the Bible. This is Luke 13:22-30: "And he went through the cities and villages, teaching, and journeying toward Jerusalem. Then said one unto him, Lord, are there few that be saved? And he said unto them, Strive to enter in at the strait gate: for many, I say unto you, will seek to enter in, and shall not be able. When once the master of the house is risen up, and hath shut to the door, and ye begin to stand without, and to knock at the door, saying, Lord, Lord, open unto us; and He shall answer and say unto you, I know you not whence ye are: Then shall ye begin to say, We have eaten and drunk in thy presence, and thou hast taught in our streets. But He shall say, I tell you, I know you not whence ye are; depart from me, all ye workers of iniquity. There shall be weeping and gnashing of teeth, when ye shall see Abraham, and Isaac, and Jacob, and all the prophets, in the kingdom of God, and you yourselves thrust out. And they shall come from the east, and from the west, and from the north, and from the south, and shall sit down in the kingdom of God. And, behold, there are last which shall be first, and there are first which shall be last. "

Okay, that was a long entry, so let's break that down into digestible chunks, yeah? The observant among you may be saying, "Well, in the earlier verse Jesus said no man cometh unto the Father but by him, right? Now this verse says the strait gate. What does strait mean?" Well, a cursory internet search shows that the third meaning of it is "narrow or confined". Isn't that interesting? There's only one way to enter the kingdom of heaven. That's to be born again by belief in Jesus's blood atonement on our behalf, hence the 'narrow' or 'strait' gate.

I believe Jesus is talking to the Jews here because of this. "We have eaten and drunk in thy presence, and thou hast taught in our streets." Also, the mention of Abraham, Isaac, and Jacob reinforces this. The Jewish people know all about Abraham, Isaac, and Jacob, but us church and the gentiles, not as much.

Did Jesus teach in Kyoto's streets? No, maybe Moscow? No? He taught in Jerusalem's streets, folks. Another reason I believe he's talking to the Jewish people here is this. "And they shall come from the east, and from the west, and from the north, and from the south, and shall sit down in the kingdom of God."

Who's that referring to? I think that's referring to us, the saints that trust in Jesus's blood, all across the globe.

Isn't that reason enough to call Jesus our blessed hope?

No? Okay, let's keep this going then. Our blessed hope refers to our escape from the tribulation. Do I have biblical backing for this claim? Oh, you bet I do. As mentioned earlier during Paul's telling of the gospel, "Moreover, brethren, I declare unto you the gospel which I preached unto you, which also ye have received, and wherein ye stand." Stand, we stand on the word of God. When in doubt, run to God's Word and read.

Let's look at what Jesus says in Luke 21:34-37: "And take heed to yourselves, lest at any time your hearts be over-charged with surfeiting, and drunkenness, and cares of this life, and so that Day come upon you unawares. For as a snare shall it come on all them that dwell on the face of the whole earth. Watch ye therefore, and pray always, that ye may be accounted worthy to **escape** all these things that shall come to pass, and to stand before the Son of man."

I believe he's saying to watch for his first return in the clouds here. We're to watch and be aware that he's coming back to fetch his church. Heck, there's even more corroboration here in 1st Thessalonians 5:1-11: "But of the times and the seasons, brethren, ye have no need that I write unto you. For yourselves know perfectly that the day of the Lord so cometh as a thief in the night. For when they shall say, Peace and safety; then sudden destruction cometh upon them, as travail upon a woman with child; and they shall not escape. But ye, brethren, are not in darkness, that that day should overtake you as a thief. Ye are all the children of light, and the children of the day: we are not of the night, nor of darkness. Therefore let us not sleep, as do others; but let us watch and be sober. For they that sleep sleep in the night;

and they that be drunken are drunken in the night. But let us, who are of the day, be sober, putting on the breastplate of faith and love; and for an helmet, the hope of salvation. For God hath not appointed us to wrath, but to obtain salvation by our Lord Jesus Christ, Who died for us, that, whether we wake or sleep, we should live together with him. Wherefore comfort yourselves together, and edify one another, even as also ye do."

Notice how in that entry, that Paul said we (born-again believers) are not appointed to God's wrath? We know Paul is speaking to born-again believers because he addresses them as brethren, aka brothers and sisters. Other born-again believers are our brothers and sisters in Christ, though sometimes online in various comment sections you wouldn't know it based on how some act and treat others, admittedly.

Here's another verse I believe refers to the Lord's appearing in the clouds. It's Titus 2:11-13: "For the grace of God that bringeth salvation hath appeared to all men, Teaching us that, denying ungodliness and worldly lusts, we should live soberly, righteously, and godly, in this present world; Looking for that blessed hope, and the glorious appearing of the great God and our Saviour Jesus Christ."

It seems obvious the Lord's appearing in the clouds and when he steps foot onto the Mount of Olives are two different instances, isn't it? This is a joyous revelation because many people think we must endure the seven years tribulation, otherwise known as Jacob's trouble. In the Bible, Jacob usually refers either to the man, Jacob, or to Israel as a whole. It's obvious Jacob's trouble refers to Israel, and that fits considering the entire point of the rapture is so that God can focus on Israel again without worrying about us born again believers being down here in the proverbial crossfire.

Also, this whole receiving us unto himself thing has deep roots in the Jewish wedding ceremony. In fact, here's Revelations 19:7-9: Let us be glad and rejoice, and give honour to him: for the marriage of the Lamb is come, and his wife hath made herself ready. And to her was granted that she should be arrayed in fine linen, clean and white: for the fine linen is the righteousness of saints. And he saith unto me, Write, Blessed *are* they which are called unto the marriage supper of the Lamb. And he saith unto me, These are the true sayings of God.

I believe the Wedding Supper of the Lamb is where we raptured saints are united with God in heaven during those seven years of Jacob's trouble. The white linen we're wearing, as it says, is Christ's righteousness (for we have none of our own).

Now, I don't know the day or hour of the rapture. Sure, I have my guesses, but don't put your faith in a date, folks. Put your faith in Christ's atoning blood and watch for that wondrous day. Here's another key rapture verse that should uplift your spirit and encourage you.

Here's 1st Corinthians 15: 51-57: "Behold, I shew you a mystery; We shall not all sleep, but we shall all be changed, In a moment, in the twinkling of an eye, at the last trump: for the trumpet shall sound, and the dead shall be raised incorruptible, and we shall be changed. For this corruptible must put on incorruption, and this mortal must put on immortality. So when this corruptible shall have put on incorruption, and this mortal shall have put on immortality, then shall be brought to pass the saying that is written, Death is swallowed up in victory. O death, where is thy sting? O grave, where is thy victory? The sting of death is sin; and the strength of sin is the law. But thanks be to God, which giveth us the victory through our Lord Jesus Christ."

That's encouraging to me at least. That's explicit in how the entire process will work. We'll be changed in a nanosecond and become immortal to raise into the clouds and meet our Lord in the air. What a blessed and wondrous day that will be. The best part? I'm pretty sure that day is very near.

Hold on to our Blessed Hope, folks. Cling to Jesus now more than ever. Keep your gaze fixed on him and don't let people demoralize you or shake your faith. Stand firm on the Word of God and His promises.

3

3: WHAT ABOUT WORKS?

Alright, fine. Let's address the elephant in the room that I'm sure somebody's itching to cry out about. It's the mainstream view nowadays that you're saved by your works. Surely you've heard the false gospel of, "You must repent of your sins to be saved!" They certainly don't hide it anymore. Never mind the fact that repentance doesn't mean feeling terrible about your sins and turning away from them. Repentance in the Bible means you should change your mind. In this case, from trusting in yourself for salvation, to trusting Jesus.

How do I know this about repentance? Okay. For context, this is where Nineveh turned from their sins as Jonah warned that Nineveh would be overthrown in 40 days. Here's Jonah 3:10: "And God saw their **works**, that they **turned from their evil way**; and God repented of the evil, that he had said that he would do unto them; and he did it not."

Repent in the Bible means to change your mind. Or if you prefer the Greek translations, it's "metanoia" - aka to change your mind about something. It's crystal clear, isn't it?

As evidenced clearly in Jonah 3:10, turning from sins is a WORK.

Turning from sin is ideal, but it indeed is a WORK. We know works are not what saves us. Our **eternal souls** are saved by belief in **Jesus's sacrificial blood atonement** and subsequent **resurrection.**

Returning to the "Turn from your sins to be saved" false gospel, it used to be you'd rarely hear this combination of words together, but nowadays? It's widespread. Those words are never found together in the Bible for a reason. Notice how it takes the focus off Jesus' blood atoning sacrifice and onto YOU. How good are YOU? What did YOU do? How much are YOU obeying the laws given to Moses? Jesus deserves all the glory – not us. Here's a verse clarifying for those who wish to put themselves under the law for their salvation. Here's Galatians 3:10: "For as many as are of the **works** of the law are under the curse: for it is written, Cursed is every one that continueth not in all things which are written in the book of the law to do them."

Aka, if you want to put yourself under the yolk of the law, you're cursed since you must follow and obey every single one. That's admittedly a weak translation, but it gets the point across.

I'm merely scratching the surface, but do you see the problem with this line of thinking? It's not about us and our supposed "righteousness". It's about being cloaked in Christ's perfect righteousness.

A lot of work salvation enthusiasts say, "Works are fruit of the spirit." Maybe they'll imply that if you're saved, you'll have works (Aka "fruits") to show your salvation. Is that what the Bible says? Here's Galatians 5:22: But the fruit of the Spirit is love, joy, peace, longsuffering, gentleness, goodness, faith, Meekness, temperance: against such there is no law.

So clearly, the fruit is not our works or our 'holy' living. It's how we act and treat others.

Here's Romans 10:1-4: "Brethren, my heart's desire and prayer to God for Israel is, that they might be saved. For I bear them record that they have a zeal of God, but not according to knowledge. For they being ignorant of God's righteousness, and going about to establish their own righteousness, have not submitted themselves unto the righteousness of God. For Christ is the end of the law for righteousness to every one that believeth."

Now, Paul was talking about Israel in Romans 10:1-4, true. Doesn't the same lesson apply to us too? Should we not learn the same lesson? What does "establishing our own righteousness" mean?

Simple, really. It means that you try to work and prove yourself righteous by obeying the law. How does one attempt such an impossible task? Well, usually this means trying to follow not just the Ten Commandments of Moses, but also the entire Mosaic Law. That totals, I believe, over 600 laws!

Remember this verse from James 2:10: "For whosoever shall keep the whole law, and yet offend in one point, he is guilty of all."

Now, many try to point at James 2:17-19 for their works-based salvation. Those read as follows. "Even so faith, if it hath not works, is dead, being alone. Yea, a man may say, Thou hast faith, and I have works: shew me thy faith without thy works, and I will shew thee my faith by my works. Thou believest that there is one God; thou doest well: the devils also believe, and tremble."

For the record, Christ's sacrifice was for mankind, not

demon kind. So, trying to disprove salvation through faith and belief in Jesus's blood atonement using this verse is outright silly given the context.

Now, let's keep reading in that very chapter, shall we? Let's check verse 23. "And the scripture was fulfilled which saith, Abraham believed God, and it was imputed unto him for righteousness: and he was called the Friend of God."

Oh dear, belief again? It's almost like there's a common theme here, huh? False teachers love to do what we in the writing business call "cherry-picking" verses and twisting them to fit their pre-conceived notions that they need to 'earn' their salvation.

Now what did James mean? Well, context is important here. Just before in James 2: 14-16 it's pretty clear. "What doth it profit, my brethren, though a man say he hath faith, and have not works? Can faith save him? If a brother or sister be naked, and destitute of daily food, And one of you say unto them, Depart in peace, be ye warmed and filled; notwithstanding ye give them not those things which are needful to the body; what doth it profit?"

Meaning that you are not profitable unto Christ if you don't show your faith to men. It's NOT saying that you're saved if you do works. It's that you're not helping the unsaved men and women. They'll look at you and go, "He's not even helping that poor beggar, and I'm supposed to believe his preaching about this Jesus fellow?" It justifies you in the eyes of men, not the Lord above.

See, even earlier in that chapter, James references a specific incident in James 2:6: "But ye have despised the poor. Do not rich men oppress you, and draw you before the judgment seats?"

So, the folks James is addressing are NOT doing these good works. That's clear, yes? Well, check verses 1 through 4 of chapter 2 and read more about who he's addressing here. It reads as such: "My brethren, have not the faith of our Lord Jesus Christ, the Lord of glory, with respect of persons. For if there come unto your assembly a man with a gold ring, in goodly apparel, and there come in also a poor man in vile raiment; And ye have respect to him that weareth the gay clothing, and say unto him, Sit thou here in a good place; and say to the poor, Stand thou there, or sit here under my footstool:"

There's that mention of brethren again. You notice that? That means he's speaking to SAVED believers. Don't believe me? Let's go back even further to James 1:18. It reads: "Of His own will begat he us with the word of truth, that we should be a kind of firstfruits of his creatures."

"Of his own will begat he us." That's certainly a unique way of wording it, but I'll interpret for those who are unfamiliar with the word begat. Beget is an "archaic" form of the word beget. What's beget mean? Here's the textbook definition. "(especially of a male parent) to procreate or generate (offspring)." This is an admittedly weak translation but essentially "Of God's will, we're his children."

That means that the people James is referring to are God's children. We've already established you cannot lose your salvation, period. Full stop. So, in my opinion, James is saying, "You're children of God; act like it to bring yet more lost souls into our fold."

Now, I'm not denying that we should do good works. Far from it. It's profitable to us, God, and those we help. It is NOT a salvation issue though, folks. People love to mix works with grace.

Here's a Bible verse that clears it up. This is Romans 11:5-6: "Even so then at this present time also there is a remnant according to the election of grace. And if by grace, then is it no more of works: otherwise grace is no more grace. But if it be of works, then is it no more grace: otherwise work is no more work."

This means it's an "either or" situation. You can try to earn (and fail) your salvation, or you can rely upon our Lord's bountiful grace for your salvation. It cannot be mixed. If you choose grace, it's no more of works. If you pick works, it's not grace, basically.

Or we could go to Ephesians 2:8-9: "For by grace are ye saved through faith; and that not of yourselves: it is the gift of God: Not of works, lest any man should boast."

Let's grab one more to really hammer the point home, shall we? Here's Galatians 5:4: "Christ is become of no effect unto you, whosoever of you are justified by the law; ye are fallen from grace."

Have I belabored the point enough? The reason God's word repeats this so often is because it's crucial to everyone here on Earth. If we take the wrong path and try to establish our own righteousness by works, AKA works-based salvation, then you're on the broad road leading to destruction as referenced in Matthew 7:13-14: "Enter ye in at the strait (narrow) gate: for wide is the gate, and broad is the way, that leadeth to destruction, and many there be which go in thereat: Because strait is the gate, and narrow is **the way**, which leadeth unto life, and few there be that find it."

Remember that **Jesus is the way**, the truth, and the life, as mentioned in John 14:6: "Jesus saith unto him, I am the **way**, the truth, and the life: no man cometh unto the Father, but by me."

Meaning, you can't reconcile your sin with the Lord by yourself and what you do, period. You and I both need Jesus' blood atonement for our sins. That's the end of the matter.

4

4: SHOULD WE DO GOOD WORKS?

Absolutely, we should. Often when brothers and sisters in Christ proclaim the gospel of God's grace, we're met with certain replies.

One of these accusations is, "Oh, you free grace believers are just looking for a license to sin. You want to be lazy and not work!"

For the record, Paul himself was accused of this same thing. Oh, how human history repeats itself. Here's his response in Romans 6:1-7: "What shall we say then? Shall we continue in sin, that grace may abound? God forbid. How shall we, that are dead to sin, live any longer therein? Know ye not, that so many of us as were baptized into Jesus Christ were baptized into his death? Therefore we are buried with him by baptism into death: that like as Christ was raised up from the dead by the glory of the Father, even so we also should walk in newness of life. For if we have been planted together in the likeness of his death, we shall be also in the likeness of his resurrection: Knowing this, that our old man is crucified with him, that the body of sin might be destroyed, that henceforth we should not serve sin. For he that is dead is freed from sin."

What's all that mean? It means that when Christ bled, died, and was buried, we were buried alongside him. That's what baptism symbolizes - that we died and were reborn with him. The old man or woman is dead, and thus we've been freed from sin. It's also a public declaration that we're saved by Jesus's blood atonement for the world to see.

Does that mean we'll never sin again in this mortal life? Oh my, no. Despite my best efforts, I sin every day. It's how it is, always has been. Some may deceive themselves and proclaim that they're sinless. Heck, I heard one gentleman claim he "hadn't sinned in over 40 years." Do you believe him? I don't. That guy got furious when the pastor called him out and had to be held back from punching him, at least according to the pastor's retelling. Here's 1st John 1:8-10: "If we say that we have no sin, we deceive ourselves, and the truth is not in us. If we confess our sins, he is faithful and just to forgive us our sins, and to cleanse us from all unrighteousness. If we say that we have not sinned, we make him a liar, and his word is not in us."

See, God's standard is perfection in all things — love, obedience, and everything else. This is in 1st John 3:15: "Whosoever hateth his brother is a murderer: and ye know that no murderer hath eternal life abiding in him."

What does that mean? It means even if you never physically harmed your brother, if you hate him, it's the same to God. A mere dirty thought counts as lust before God. At least, that's what I gather from this. See, back then folks said, "Well, I didn't murder anyone, nor did I cheat on my wife. I'm righteous, right?" The people saying this were not believers, sadly; they were followers of the law, thus not saved and still considered sinners (since they couldn't live that perfect life like Jesus). I say that because remember Galatians 2:16 again: "Knowing that a man is not justified by the works of the law, but by the **faith of Jesus Christ**, even we have believed in Jesus Christ, that we might be justified by the faith of Christ, and not by the works of the law: for **by the works of the law shall no flesh be justified.**"

Now, regarding why I believe we should indeed still do good works, alright? We've established that nobody's saved by doing these things. So why still do them? Well, one, because it pleases the Lord.

How do I know this? Matthew 6:20-21: "But lay up for yourselves treasures in heaven, where neither moth nor rust doth corrupt, and where thieves do not break through nor steal: For where your treasure is, there will your heart be also."

Jesus is our ultimate treasure, folks. I cannot stress this enough. I believe that when we do good works, we store up for ourselves treasures in heaven.

Another reason is what we learned from James earlier. If we do good works, our witness is bolstered. What does that mean? If you see a born-again believer on the street and he gives a homeless man $20 and says, "God bless you," you'd probably leave with a good impression of him, yes? You'd be more likely to listen to him since he appears to live his convictions. Where if you see a different born-again believer sneer at the homeless as they walk by, I bet your opinion would be quite different. You see what I'm getting at? That's what being profitable to your fellow man means. You're far more likely to help them understand the gospel of Christ's atonement and help lead them to the Lord that way.

Corollary to this is that good works usually make you feel positive emotions. Whether this is from the Lord, or your own conscience, I don't know. Remember the feeling when you'd help your mother when you were growing up? Sure, few of us truly wanted to, but after we did, didn't you feel better? What's that saying? Good deeds are their own reward.

Bottom line, yes, we should do good works for others. We don't do them for eternal salvation because we don't earn it. We do good works because it pleases our Lord, and it profits not just us, but those we witness too. Isn't that a worthy goal if nothing else? Why ruin our own witness and become less effective in speaking about our Lord? Remember, the Lord didn't come for the righteous down here on Earth; he came for us sinners. Never forget that caveat.

5

5: FALSE GOSPELS

Why am I writing about these? Simple, I don't want folks to fall into the same snares I and many others have. These stumbling blocks usually come about because some intellectuals get to thinking and interpreting scripture wrong, I imagine. One has to do with prioritizing money above all else, like this first one we'll talk about. These come in all shapes and sizes, and all are equally insidious.

Perhaps you've heard of some of these. I pray the church you attend doesn't espouse any of these, but in the world today, those odds are low for everyone who reads this. Odds are, someone's church does, sadly.

Alright, enough preamble, let's get into the meat and potatoes of this subject and learn about what we should mark and avoid with Bible verses to back them up. Remember, my word isn't what you should trust. It's the word of God himself, aka the Bible.

Let's start with one of the more common instances I've witnessed. Not in person, mind you, but, oh boy, it's all over the internet, radio, and television in modern day. We're starting with the prosperity gospel. Maybe you've heard of it.

This false gospel plays to our baser instincts and the way our minds work. It basically says that our prosperity and financial blessings are always God's will for his believers. Essentially, have you ever heard a preacher or pastor crow on and on about the more you give, the bigger the blessing God will bestow upon you? They usually call this seed faith or will call for you to give a monetary amount and call it planting a seed for your future.

I bet you have. Heck, I never attended these churches once, thank God, and even I have heard this countless times. They'll repeat that it's imperative that your offering be as much as you can afford for your own good. The more you give, the more God will bless you. They also usually mention that God will improve your health the more dollar bills you place into that offering plate. Boy, you should notice how often they mention that plate. They always conveniently ignore the passages in the Bible warning about the love of money.

This appeals to our baser instincts, doesn't it? It treats God more like an investment. "If I put more into this church, God will give more to me!" Sure, that SOUNDS logical, but we should remember a few important verses in God's word.

Here's Isaiah 55:9: "For as the heavens are higher than the earth, so are my ways higher than your ways, and my thoughts than your thoughts." What sounds good and logical to us isn't always how God thinks. It's important to remember that. We're also NOT promised an easy life in scripture. In fact, it's quite the opposite. I don't remember ever reading a verse that promised that if you gave more cash that you received an easier time, do you?

In fact, Here's Luke 12:13-21: "And one of the company said unto him, Master, speak to my brother, that he divide the inheritance with me. And he said unto him, Man, who made me a judge or a divider over you? And he said unto them, Take heed, and beware of covetousness: for a man's life consisteth not in the abundance of the things which he possesseth. And he spake a parable unto them, saying, The ground of a certain rich man brought forth plentifully: And he thought within himself, saying, What shall I do, because I have no room where to bestow my fruits? And he said, This will I do: I will pull down my barns, and build greater; and there will I bestow all my fruits and my goods. And I will say to my soul, Soul, thou hast much goods laid up for many years; take thine ease, eat, drink, and be merry. But God said unto him, Thou fool, this night thy soul shall be required of thee: then whose shall those things be, which thou hast provided? So is he that layeth up treasure for himself, and is not rich toward God."

That was a mouthful. I believe this essentially was a warning for those who prioritize wealth and possessions over the Lord himself. Oh, there's more too. Here's another in 1st Timothy 6:6-10: "But godliness with contentment is great gain. For we brought nothing into this world, and it is certain we can carry nothing out. And having food and raiment let us be therewith content. But they that will be rich fall into temptation and a snare, and into many foolish and hurtful lusts, which drown men in destruction and perdition. For the love of money is the root of all evil: which while some coveted after, they have erred from the faith, and pierced themselves through with many sorrows."

Or how about that rich man who asked Jesus about eternal life? Remember him in Mark: 10: 17-22: "And when he was gone forth into the way, there came one running, and kneeled to him, and asked him, Good Master, what shall I do that I may inherit eternal life? And Jesus said unto him, Why callest thou me good? there is none good but one, that is, God. Thou knowest the commandments, Do not commit adultery, Do not kill, Do not steal, Do not bear false witness, Defraud not, Honour thy father and mother. And he answered and said unto him, Master, all these have I observed from my youth. Then Jesus beholding him loved him, and said unto him, One thing thou lackest: go thy way, sell whatsoever thou hast, and give to the poor, and thou shalt have treasure in heaven: and come, take up the cross, and follow me. And he was sad at that saying, and went away grieved: for he had great possessions."

This passage shows that the wealthy man approached Jesus with a law-based salvation mindset, and that's why Jesus told him to sell everything and follow him. Notice how Jesus told him that nobody is good except God. A subtle "You haven't lived a perfect life free from sin." The young man thought he kept the whole law, and Jesus proved to him he hadn't using the law. This also is a reminder that wealth can cause other sins, like idolatry. He didn't want to give up his money, did he? Who does, right? Not me, that's for sure. Thankfully, I don't rely on the law for my salvation.

Time and time again we see in the Bible that we're not guaranteed wealth, and often it can be detrimental. Am I saying we have to be poor? Not at all. Just that wealth has its own set of temptations, and we should be mindful of where we put our faith and trust. We don't trust in our riches to secure blessings and salvation. We trust Jesus and his atoning blood and sacrifice.

I've also heard some of these prosperity gospel preachers lead their congregations in what they call the "sinner's prayer". They said something like, "Repeat after me and you'll be saved."

Is uttering a prayer how we're saved? You can be saved during a prayer, yes, but the prayer itself isn't how we're saved. We're only saved by belief in Jesus' perfect atonement for our sins on the cross, not by merely repeating words spoken by a charismatic pastor.

Here's one more for the road for the 'prosperity gospel' in Hebrews 13:5: "Let your conversation be without covetousness; and be content with such things as ye have: for he hath said, I will never leave thee, nor forsake thee."

Mind you, that's just ONE false gospel. Buckle up, folks. We're just starting.

Works based false gospels

Yes, we've sort of already addressed this, but it needs reiteration and extrapolation. Why? Because it's so overly pervasive anymore and insidious in its methods.

Purveyors of this gospel often love to say, "Yes, we're saved by God's Grace through faith, BUT our works prove we're saved."

Hmm. Is that what the Bible says, though? Or is that human reasoning? I'm betting it's the latter.

What does that simple addition to the gospel mean? Well, take away the works part of the equation. In their view, if you do no works, what does that mean for you? By their definition, if you take away your works, you're not saved. That's the math equation, isn't it? If works supposedly prove you're saved and you don't do them, what's that mean? Doesn't that mean that their path to salvation is by works by their own admission? See, many of them will pay lip service to God's bountiful grace and that we should have faith, but they always have to sneak in that works to prove you're saved bit.

I'm sure what I'm saying is making a few froth at the

mouth, but it's true, and I cannot stand idly by and not say anything.

Yes, we should do good works, and I mentioned that in a previous chapter. No, it doesn't prove that you, me, or your mother is saved.

I fell because of this stumbling block for a little while. Let me tell you, it saps away your assurance. You're constantly wondering. "Am I saved? I mean, I didn't do that good work today. Does that mean I've lost my salvation? Was I ever really saved, since I didn't do this work?"

Assurance of salvation is crucial for our happiness, and God knows it. Why do you think he repeats that if we believe in Jesus' finished work on the cross, that we're heaven bound? I believe it's so we can have assurance and happiness down here. So, we can rest in the Lord. Here's Psalms 37:7: "Rest in the LORD, and wait patiently for him: fret not thyself because of him who prospereth in his way, because of the man who bringeth wicked devices to pass."

Yes, many of these works-based salvation types teach the loss of salvation. In fact, they say. "OSAS (Once saved, always saved) is a doctrine of devils and from the pits of hell!" Often if in text form, this proclamation is in all capital letters, implying they're yelling it.

As one pastor I've listened to said. "If you can lose salvation, you've lost it." This is because we all live in sin in some form or another. Maybe you stub your toe, and a curse word comes out. Maybe you notice an attractive member of the opposite sex and your mind wonders to lascivious subject matters. Perhaps you see a news story of something heinous, and you grow angry at the terrible thing that happened. It doesn't matter. The point is all have fallen short of the glory of God, besides Jesus, obviously.

Many who practice this work-based salvation love saying, "If you're saved, you must be obedient and prove you're really saved." In their minds, that means following all God's laws to "prove" you're saved and wasn't a "false convert".

However, remember we've already established that nobody's saved by the law. It only condemns. Remember Galatians 3:11: "But that no man is justified by the law in the sight of God, it is evident: for, The just shall live by faith."

Just earlier in Galatians 3:2-5: "This only would I learn of you, Received ye the Spirit by the works of the law, or by the hearing of faith? Are ye so foolish? having begun in the Spirit, are ye now made perfect by the flesh? Have ye suffered so many things in vain? if it be yet in vain. He therefore that ministereth to you the Spirit, and worketh miracles among you, doeth he it by the works of the law, or by the hearing of faith?"

Do you see the point of this? Works, aka the law, cannot save us or prove we're saved. That's not how that works. We're to place faith in the Lord Jesus Christ and His atoning work. We prove we're saved by believing the gospel of salvation. You know you're saved, because you believe and trust God's word. Period, full stop.

You'll notice if someone genuinely asks these sorts of preachers, "What must I do to be saved?" They'll never have a simple answer.

Heck, I won't mention names, but I watched this very interaction with a very famous so-called pastor, and it went a little something like this.

The young lady stood up after being called on from the congregation and cleared her throat.

"Yes, miss?" the man asked.

"What must I do to be saved?"

The man smirked and beckoned her up onto the stage

and waited until she stood before the entire mega church. "Do you love God?" he asked.

The young lady seemed visibly nervous and clearly uncomfortable in front of this giant crowd. She fidgeted and kept her eyes on the floor near her feet. "Yes."

The man leaned against the pulpit. "Do you turn from sin?" he asked.

She took a moment and answered in a small voice, in an almost question. "I try to?"

"Do you hate sin?" he asked.

"Yes."

"Have you called out to God and pleaded with him to save you from the fires of hell?"

You get the point I trust. Not once did he simply ask, "Do you believe Jesus died, bled for our atonement, was buried and resurrected on the third day according to the scriptures?"

Not once did he mention any of that. Sure, that young lady may have gone home that night and felt all nice and secure, but do you truly think that feeling lasted? I'm betting she went home and did something naughty eventually and then felt terrible. She likely doubted her own salvation afterward, right?

You know why? He asked about her. Did YOU do this? Did YOU do that? Have YOU done this other work? It took the focus off Jesus and onto her, an imperfect human. If we have to rely on ourselves and we inherently know that we're sinners, what assurance does that grant?

Absolutely zero whatsoever. How can you rely on yourself and your righteousness if you have none? If you have no assurance, you won't be happy in this life. Rest in God's word, folks, for your own happiness.

I think I've made my point.

The bloodless gospel:

This false gospel is subtle, and that's what makes it so dangerous. Proponents of this false gospel will say almost verbatim: "It's not Christ's blood that saves. It was his death."

On the surface, that sounds almost plausible to the human mind, doesn't it? See, the problem was as I mentioned earlier.

"How that Christ died."

Did Jesus drown in the Sea of Galilee? No, he didn't. Did he die of heatstroke? Of course not. Are we singing hymns at church about when Jesus had a heart attack? Obviously not. He had nails driven into various parts of his body after being whipped mercilessly and had a crown of thorns thrust onto his head. Then he hung there on a cross, bleeding out in front of a crowd.

Here's Hebrews: 9:22: "And almost all things are by the law purged with blood; and **without shedding of blood is no remission."**

That means that things of the law (aka sin when we break the law) are purged with blood. Without the shedding of blood, there is no remission (to release from the guilt or penalty of).

Seems clear cut, doesn't it?

I've actually heard so-called pastors say something like, "It's not Jesus's blood. It's not magic blood that clears us from our sins."

Hmm, what do you think? Do you trust God's word? Or do you trust man's reasoning about God and how he works? I don't know about you, but I'll trust in my Lord, thanks. Heck, in this very session of typing this, I found quite a few websites all proclaiming it's not Jesus' blood that washes us clean. They claim it's only his death and that traditional views are 'outdated' or 'based in pagan practices'. It's a sad state of the world. It couldn't be that pagans saw the truth and implemented that practice into their own cults, huh? No, according to many, the pagans made it first, clearly. Yes, that was sarcasm before someone thinks I'm serious.

I guess they just didn't remember that one little word in the gospel. 1st Corinthians 15:1-4: "Moreover, brethren, I declare unto you the gospel which I preached unto you, which also ye have received, and wherein ye stand; By which also ye are saved, if ye keep in memory what I preached unto you, unless ye have believed in vain. For I delivered unto you first of all that which I also received, **how** that Christ died for our sins according to the scriptures; And that he was buried, and that he rose again the third day according to the scriptures."

Here's another very clear and candid verse in Leviticus 17:11: "For the life of the flesh is in the blood: and I have given it to you upon the altar to make an atonement for your souls: for it is the **blood** that maketh an atonement for the soul."

There's not much room for "interpretation" there. It's clear; blood must be spilled for forgiveness of sins. In our case, that's Jesus's precious blood on the cross that paid for our iniquities. That's exactly why he's called the "**Lamb of God**."

You want more? Okay, remember Exodus? Do you know what Passover is? Where God smote the firstborn of Egypt? It's not popular, but it reinforces this obvious point.

In that recollection, Moses informs the Hebrew people how to be safe from this plague. Here's Exodus 12:21-23: "Then Moses called for all the elders of Israel, and said unto them, Draw out and take you a **lamb** according to your families, and kill the passover. And ye shall take a bunch of hyssop, and dip it in the blood that is in the bason, and strike the lintel and the two side posts with the blood that is in the bason; and none of you shall go out at the door of his house until the morning. For the LORD will pass through to smite the Egyptians; and when he seeth the blood upon the lintel, and on the two side posts, the LORD will pass over the door, and will not suffer the destroyer to come in unto your houses to smite you."

This kept the Hebrews safe from their first borne being taken.

There is power in the blood, folks. Never forget that.

In case you need yet another confirmation that I'm not blowing smoke, here's Romans 5:8-11: "But God commendeth his love toward us, in that, while we were yet sinners, Christ died for us. Much more then, being now **justified by his blood**, we shall be saved from wrath through him. For if, when we were enemies, we were reconciled to God by the death of his Son, much more, being reconciled, we shall be saved by his life. And not only so, but we also joy in God through our Lord Jesus Christ, by whom we have now received the atonement."

If you still don't get it, go back and pay special attention to the bold words and pray for understanding from the Holy Spirit. I imagine you won't need to, though.

There are likely more false gospels that I'm not familiar with, but remember to stand on God's word, not men's ideas. When in doubt, default to God's perfect word.

Lordship Salvation

Yes, we need to speak of this group too. This group thinks you have to 'make Jesus the Lord and master of your life'.

Boy, talk about ego, huh? "Make Jesus Lord?" He is Lord already! He always has been. Now, I realize they're probably saying to prioritize Jesus, but isn't that simply just discipleship? You don't need to follow in discipleship to be saved. We should pick up our cross and follow in discipleship after we're saved, yes, but it's not required for salvation. Salvation and discipleship are two different concepts. You get saved first, and THEN we can engage in discipleship.

This group believes that the "proof" of your salvation is how you live your life, the same as the works trusters. At least, from my understanding of it. According to a prominent figure who recently passed, he said this: "The gospel call to faith presupposes that sinners must repent of their sin and yield to Christ's authority."

In other words, they don't understand how the word "repent" is used in the Bible. They believe you must turn from your sins (a work) to be saved.

Now, where have we heard what repent means before? Oh, right here in Jonah 3:10: "And God saw their works, that they turned from their evil way; and **God repented** of the evil, that he had said that he would do unto them; and he did it not."

In other words, God changed his mind, not turned from sin. Do these folks think God can sin? I've never once heard these types ever address that verse or others like it. God repented thirty something times in the Bible. (I'm unaware of the exact number.) I wonder what they make of that.

Here's the skinny. God is perfect in all ways, those we can comprehend, and especially in those beyond our grasp. He does not sin and is always righteous, period.

6

6: ONCE SAVED, ALWAYS SAVED?

Yes, once we're saved, we're always saved. Chapter over.

Oh, you want a little more explanation? I feel we've already done this, but for the sake of the lost, I'll try my best with the good Lord's help.

Let's start with Ephesians 4:30: "And grieve not the holy Spirit of God, whereby ye are sealed unto the day of redemption."

What's sealed mean in this instance? The sealing represents security and ownership. Basically, it's saying that you're eternally secure. It's a sort of guarantor of inheritance, an assurance if you will.

This means once you're saved by believing in the atoning blood of Jesus Christ, you're set for eternity. You're his son or daughter, and his Holy Spirit dwells within you. It encourages us believers to live with confidence and trust that we're God's precious children.

Let me ask you a question. If you have three teenage children, and let's say you take them with you to the mall. You tell them to meet you at a specific spot at an appointed time since they're old enough to walk around unsupervised.

That appointed time came, and one of the three obeyed and arrived on time.

What do you do? Do you say, 'Eh, who cares? Those two didn't obey me perfectly. They're not my children anymore.'?

Who in the world would? What parent would disown a child over mere disobedience? Once they're your child, they're always your child.

It seems to me that some folks simply misunderstand God's character. Maybe I'm wrong, but it seems too many people view God as some sort of angry schoolteacher who's a real stickler for the rules. You know the type, the ones who look for reasons to get you in trouble because it amuses them. We all had one in school, but that's not God. Imagine this nonsensical example and truly ask yourself if it makes any sense that a perfectly righteous and sinless God would do this.

Imagine God sitting on his throne, and he speaks. "Oh, did you see that, Gabriel? John Doe down there committed adultery in his mind. Erase him from the Lamb's Book of Life right now! No, I know I said he's sealed until the day of redemption since he believed on my Son's precious blood, but that's the last straw. I changed my mind!"

Do you or anyone seriously believe that God is like that? No, he's not a liar. If he says we're sealed until the day of redemption, then buckle your seatbelt and get comfortable, because you're with him forever, thank the Lord.

Now, I realize I'm biased. In my previous book, I detailed my near-death experience and my encounter with our Heavenly Father.

For those who haven't read "My Visit to Heaven," then here's a quick refresher. I suffocated, everything went black, and I woke up in a blackened tunnel being carried by what I thought to be an angel. We approached the brightest light I've ever seen until we were engulfed, and next thing I knew, I was in the most beautiful garden I've ever experienced. I saw colors I've never encountered on Earth, waterfalls as far as the eye can see, perfect flowers not found here.

Perfect love washed over me, a feeling of security, that everything would be alright. If I asked a question, the answer was immediately given to me, presumably from the Holy Spirit. I felt completely safe, loved, and adored. Then I heard our Father's voice behind me.

I stumbled to my feet and turned to face him. All I saw was a blinding light. I couldn't see hands, feet, his head, or anything. He asked me if I had the choice, would I stay there with him, or would I choose to go back to my family on Earth. You know what I said? "I want to stay here with you, Father, please!"

Unfortunately, he saw it wasn't yet my time, and so I started begging Him to let me stay there with Him. The angel from before must've taken that as his cue, because he/she grabbed me from behind and dragged me back the way we came until I was thrown into my body again.

I know for a fact that God loves every one of us more than we can even imagine. You can feel it in His very presence! I can't explain it better. When you're near Him, love, security, warmth, blinding light, and peace radiate off Him! So, seeing people mis-characterize Him breaks my heart. Sure, he's righteous and perfectly just. We must remember he's also the God of love, grace, and mercy too.

His strength is perfected in our weakness. This is referenced from 2nd Corinthians 12:9: "And he said unto me, My grace is sufficient for thee: for my strength is made perfect in weakness. Most gladly therefore will I rather glory in my infirmities, that the power of Christ may rest upon me."

One of God's many strengths is His grace. You know, that wondrous mercy that so many want to deny the power of.

I've actually heard folks say such things like, "Jesus did his part. You have to do yours too, or you're not saved." Or, another thing I've heard is, "God's mercy is not infinite for his children, and eventually he'll cast you out of his hand. He didn't say he couldn't drop you!" Another variant of this is the following. "Jesus may have said no man can pluck you from the Father's hand, but he never said you couldn't jump out."

Like, are you serious? You don't think you yourself are a man? What part of, "No man can pluck you out of the Father's hand" is difficult to grasp here? Sounds like they're denying God's grace and saying it's not enough for us. I'm flabbergasted why so many are quick to throw away the one lifeline we have. Why on Earth?

God's grace is all we have to rely on, folks. If we can lose our salvation, is that even grace? Sounds more conditional to me. Aka, you have to earn that salvation. **Grace is unearned favor.**

Imagine you have a child, and your toddler does something really hurtful. Maybe they yell "I hate you" when they're having a fit. Maybe they kick you or something equally harmful. You still love them since they're your baby. I've heard people say, "I don't care that you're 30 years old, you're still my baby boy!"

Imagine how God sees us. He's always been, is, and always shall be. Even if we're 80 years old, he still sees us as his little babies. He's the perfect Father, and we should try to understand that.

Now I can see some folks' replies already. "Sounds like you just want to live the way you want and you're excusing sin!"

I'm not saying to go forth and sin as you see fit. We should want to try to avoid sin, true. If nothing else, because we know it would grieve the Holy Spirit. We don't want to grieve God, right? Remember 1st Thessalonians 5:19: "Quench not the Spirit."

We obey to show our love to our Father, not to 'get or prove we're really saved.' Or as I've heard from a brother in Christ, Tom, "We get to go to church, not we have to." Same principle. Does he want us to attend church, to treat each other with love, and to pray for our enemies? Absolutely.

You never want to make your dear mother or father down here on Earth sad, do you? What child tries to make their parents cry? Perhaps in anger you might, but that's hardly you in your right mind, correct?

We in the body of Christ should edify, build each other up, and encourage each other. Instead, what do we see online?

Fear-mongering, tearing each other down, and squabbling are what I see across the internet. It's not everywhere, granted, but boy is it common.

It could be the most encouraging and edifying video of all time, and without a doubt, you will almost always see at least one comment saying something like, "You hyper grace believers think you can enter the kingdom of heaven with your habitual sinful lifestyles? You're delusional, and you have a nasty surprise when you and those you lead into hell realize your error!"

They might throw in a cherry-picked verse that's completely out of context to try to support their accusation. Usually this is James 2:17: "Even so faith, if it hath not works, is dead, being alone." Mind you, they usually don't even quote the verse correctly. It's always "Faith without works is dead!" or "Even the devils believe and tremble!" Context? What's that? No thank you, they must say.

As I mentioned earlier, Jesus' atonement wasn't for the devils; it was for us sinful humans! Remember back in Chapter 3, where we dissected this very set of verses? Go back and read it if you've forgotten. I won't repeat myself needlessly and bog this down.

Another verse they love to throw out is Hebrews 10:26: "For if we sin wilfully after that we have received the knowledge of the truth, there remaineth no more sacrifice for sins."

Now, never mind the fact that this was written to the Hebrews, but this isn't saying what they claim I believe. Not sure if you know, but Orthodox Jewish folks don't believe Jesus is their Messiah. That's the truth I believe that verse is referring to. The knowledge of the truth is Jesus' crucifixion and his bearing of our sins. I believe that verse is saying, "There's no more animal sacrifices for sins because Jesus already paid for those with his perfect blood."

Since I'm on a roll, why not continue? Another verse they love to pluck out of context is potentially the scariest words in the Bible, if you don't understand it. Here's Matthew 7:21-23: "Not every one that saith unto me, Lord, Lord, shall enter into the kingdom of heaven; but he that doeth the will of my Father which is in heaven. Many will say to me in that day, Lord, Lord, have we not prophesied in thy name? and in thy name have cast out devils? and in thy name done many wonderful **works**? And then will I profess unto them, I never knew you: depart from me, ye that work iniquity."

Works trusters will often quote this verse to 'prove' you can lose your salvation. That you need more works and to live holy, because to them, the will of the Father is obedience. What do those verses really say? Untwist those verses from their hands and let's decipher it with the lens of scripture, shall we?

"Not every one that saith unto me, Lord, Lord, shall enter into the kingdom of heaven; but he that doeth the will of my Father which is in heaven."

What's the will of the father? Is it "Live a holy life and do not sin?" Do you remember? The Bible clarified this with crystal clear language earlier. Here's John 6:39-40 with Jesus speaking again. "And this is the Father's will which hath sent me, that of all which he hath given me **I should lose nothing,** but should raise it up again at the last day. And this is the will of him that sent me, that every one which seeth the Son, and **believeth** on him, may have everlasting life: and I will raise him up at the last day."

It's clear that it's God's will that Jesus would lose none of his sheep.

Remember John 10:27-30? It reads: "My sheep hear my voice, and I know them, and they follow me: And I give unto them eternal life; and they shall never perish, nether shall any man pluck them out of my hand. My father, which gave them me, is greater than all; and no man is able to pluck them out of my Father's hand. I and my Father are one."

Now let's continue dissecting Matthew 7:21-23.

"Many will say to me Lord, Lord, have we not prophesied in thy name? and in thy name cast out devils? And in thy name done many wonderful **works**?"

Hmm. To justify why Jesus should open the door, what did these people point to? That's correct. They pointed at their works (good deeds, etc.) that they've done. They didn't trust in Jesus's blood atonement; they trusted in their own works!

The last sentence is self-explanatory. He orders them to

leave and calls them workers of iniquity. Aka, they never followed His will to believe on His Son's sacrificial blood atonement on their behalf.

Here's clarification for why God doesn't accept our good works for righteousness. Here's Isaiah 64:6: "But we are all as an unclean thing, and all our righteousnesses are as filthy rags; and we all do fade as a leaf; and our iniquities, like the wind, have taken us away."

I'm so weary of accusations and nastiness. Personally, I wish I didn't feel led to make this public rebuke, but I do. I say accusation because that's what these types of comments are. The deciphered comment reads like, "You sinners won't go to heaven like me. I'm so holy, unlike you!" Doesn't it? I don't mean to be mean or hurtful, but we are called to be honest, and that's how it sounds to me.

Mind you, I fully think they believe that they're going to heaven. For the record, I hope they accompany us skyward. I don't wish them or anyone eternal torment in the least. Sometimes they'll even admit, "Oh sure, I sin, but I repent of my sins, and I don't make a habit of living in sin."

What's their measurement for how much sin you can do without it being a habit, exactly? We'd love some hard numbers, wouldn't we? We get no answer, of course, from men, but God Almighty gave us numbers. Remember? We went over it earlier in James 2:10: "For whosoever shall keep the whole law, and yet offend in **one** point, he is guilty of all."

One. The answer is one sin, and you're condemned if you're not covered with the blood of Jesus and under his grace and mercy. That's it. Whose word are you going to take? Men's reasoning or God's promises? I'll believe God, thanks. You should too.

7

7: OBEYING CHRIST'S COMMANDS

Now, with all that said, we should try to live a holy life. This is a corollary of doing good works, but it needs mentioning. Yes, we trust in the blood of Jesus for salvation. He commands us to lead holy lives, or at least as holy of lives as we can down here. He says this in 2nd Peter 3:10-11: "But the day of the Lord will come as a thief in the night; in the which the heavens shall pass away with a great noise, and the elements shall melt with fervent heat, the earth also and the works that are therein shall be burned up. Seeing then that all these things shall be dissolved, what manner of persons ought ye to be in all holy conversation and godliness,"

We try our best to follow this command because it pleases God, helps aid our witnessing to the lost souls, and honestly can make you just plain feel better about yourself.

Some take this to the extreme, as mentioned earlier, and believe you need to do this or you're not going to heaven. I disagree with that assessment.

Do I believe we're to go out partying, doing drugs, and living a worldly life? No, I don't believe so. Is it fun to do these things? I'd be lying if I said no. I lived that life for nigh twenty years.

Am I going to go around wagging my finger at folks and accusing them of this, that, and the other thing if they do? No. Should I? I don't know. I doubt that's the correct action to take.

Here's the thing most folks forget: Until the day that trumpet sounds, we're mortal, in a corruptible shell, and have our sin nature that we fight against. Yes, we fight as best we can to not grieve the Holy Spirit, but only one man has ever lived a sinless life. Anyone who thinks they can copy Jesus' sinless life is in for an unpleasant surprise.

Don't set the standard as perfection. That will only lead to dissatisfaction and disappointment. Remember that God is omniscient and omnipresent. That means he's everywhere and knows everything. He knows when you're making an effort to please him. Maybe you fail and lose your temper, but he understands. I won't claim that the effort is purely enough, but it's the best we can do. Bottom line, we're counting on God's unearned grace for our eternal life, right? Thus, we should try to please our Father by trying to do what He's said. Will we always succeed? Oh my, no.

It's like this example: You're helping your child with their math homework. You show them the formula they need to use and, on the next problem, you let them try their best unassisted. Odds are if they're like me at that age, they won't get it right first try, maybe not even the second or third. They're attempting to copy what you did, but they can't quite remember or implement it just right. Eventually, they may learn the lesson and overcome that problem, but uh-oh, there's an entire book of unique problems with different solutions and processes to find them? What's more, every year their math textbooks will get harder and more difficult to solve. What's worse, they may even mess up down the road and get that very problem they just learned wrong because of an error!

That's likely a poor example, but hopefully you understand my point. In that example, God's the teacher, and we're the six-year-old trying to learn math. It'll take our entire lives (school) of trying to get it correct. We try, despite knowing we're going to fail, repeatedly. Why? To bring joy to God, who's given us eternal life through His mercy and His Son's blood atonement.

So yes, live as holy of a life as you can! I'm trying to do the same thing. We all have our stumbling blocks, every single one of us. For each person, they're different. For one, it's drugs, for another, it's lust. Many struggle with pride or doubt. Another might have anger problems, and so on. Instead of accusing and fear-mongering, we should edify and encourage each other. Meaning help in a kind way, not anger.

Does accusing our brothers and sisters in Christ help them live better? No. All it does is demoralize, strike fear, and sometimes instill hopelessness. Is that how'd you'd "help" your brother or sister? I sure hope not.

Now, am I a shining example of helping folks? No, I have social anxiety, social avoidance disorder (probably; I'm a hermit), but I can at least write this book to ease some worries.

Remember, even if you're not a writer, and you prefer solitude like me, we can always pray. Bring before the Lord and pray an intercessory prayer on behalf of others. As the Bible says in James 5:16: "Confess your faults one to another, and pray one for another, that ye may be healed. The effectual fervent prayer of a righteous man availeth much."

Availeth much is a fancier way of saying, "It works!"

People seem to underestimate prayer. I did for a while, but what do we have to lose by trusting God's word and trying? We have nothing to lose, and it will help our brothers and sisters. Is that not enough reason to pray for each other? Granted, my prayers likely aren't eloquent and fancy sounding, but the Bible even has verses addressing that too!

Matthew 6:7: "But when ye pray, use not vain repetitions, as the heathen do: for they think that they shall be heard for their much speaking."

Meaning, speak from your heart.

Here's 1st Timothy 2:1-5: "I exhort therefore, that, first of all, supplications, prayers, intercessions, and giving of thanks, be made for all men; For kings, and for all that are in authority; that we may lead a quiet and peaceable life in all godliness and honesty. For this is good and acceptable in the sight of God our Saviour; Who will have all men to be saved, and to come unto the knowledge of the truth. For there is one God, and one mediator between God and men, the man Christ Jesus;"

Sounds like it pleases the Lord when we pray intercessions for others, doesn't it?

Now there's also another important reason we should try to avoid sinning. You want to take a guess at what that is?

Here's a Bible verse explaining it better than I could, but I'll expound on it afterward. Here's Romans 6:23: "For the wages of sin is death; but the gift of God is eternal life through Jesus Christ our Lord."

Have you ever heard someone say, "Oh, you're saved now, you're free from sin." Technically they're correct. If you believe, you're born again in the spirit, as Jesus says. Here's John 3:3-6: "Jesus answered and said unto him, Verily, verily, I say unto thee, Except a man be born again, he cannot see the kingdom of God. Nicodemus saith unto him, How can a man be born when he is old? can he enter the second time into his mother's womb, and be born? Jesus answered, Verily, verily, I say unto thee, Except a man be born of water and of the Spirit, he cannot enter into the kingdom of God. That which is born of the flesh is flesh; and that which is born of the Spirit is spirit."

This passage has given birth to misunderstandings with men for ages. Have you ever had someone tell you that you need to be water baptized or you're not going to heaven? This series of verses is likely the reason. It's not like I don't understand HOW they came to this conclusion. "Except a man be born of water and of the Spirit, he cannot enter into the Kingdom of God." They always forget that last verse. "That which is born of the flesh is flesh; and that which is born of the Spirit is spirit."

Does that mean we NEED water baptism to enter heaven? Now, admittedly, I'm no Bible scholar, but here's my interpretation. Water baptismal regeneration (Aka water baptism required for salvation) isn't quite correct. I always understood it like this. What surrounds a baby in their mother's womb? Amniotic fluid, correct? I always understood it to mean, "Unless you were born of the flesh and the Spirit, you cannot enter the kingdom of God."

Remember the thief on the cross? Folks always forget him. Here's Luke 23:39-43: "And one of the malefactors which were hanged railed on him, saying, If thou be Christ, save thyself and us. But the other answering rebuked him, saying, Dost not thou fear God, seeing thou art in the same condemnation? And we indeed justly; for we receive the due reward of our deeds: but this man hath done nothing amiss. And he said unto Jesus, Lord, remember me when thou comest into thy kingdom. And Jesus said unto him,

Verily I say unto thee, To-day shalt thou be with me in paradise."

Do folks think the thief on the cross is in hell right now because he couldn't go get baptized? I believe Jesus' words here! It's not like he could go, "Um, hey guys, I need to get water baptized. Uh, can you like let me down and allow me passage to the river Jordan real quick? See, I need to be dunked in water before I can go to heaven." He believed in Jesus, and in that moment he was spiritually reborn!

Some claim that it was technically a different age, and that's why he didn't need to be water baptized. That reasoning is thin, and they know it.

What about those on their deathbeds who finally believe in Jesus' atonement on their behalf and that he resurrected? Are they going to hell? They're baptized in the Spirit in that moment, but because they weren't dunked in water, are they going to hell? I refuse to believe that. Our loving Father wouldn't do that.

After all, baptism is an outward expression of an inward transformation and commitment to God. Remember when Jesus got baptized?

Here's Matthew 3:16: "And Jesus, when he was baptized, went up straightway out of the water: and, lo, the **heavens were opened** unto him, and he saw the Spirit of God descending like a dove, and **lighting upon him**:"

Many think this is the verse where it confirms that we receive the Spirit after being water baptized, but I believe our spiritual baptism is when we believe. Jesus' baptism marks the beginning of His public ministry and sets an example for believers. It fulfilled Isaiah 64:1: "Oh that thou wouldest **rend the heavens**, that thou wouldest come down, that the mountains might flow down at thy presence,"

Also, Isaiah 11:2: "And **the spirit of the LORD shall rest**

upon him, the spirit of wisdom and understanding, the spirit of counsel and might, the spirit of knowledge and of the fear of the LORD;"

Lighting upon him basically means resting on him. So it was the Spirit of God fulfilling prophecy and setting an example to us, his believers. Now, back in Jesus' time on Earth, when you believed, you went to get baptized like right fricking now. It was understood that you believed; you would go do it immediately.

Now, admittedly, we SHOULD get water baptized. Jesus commands it after all. Here's Matthew 28:19-20: "Go ye therefore, and teach all nations, baptizing them in the name of the Father, and of the Son, and of the Holy Ghost: Teaching them to observe all things whatsoever I have commanded you: and, lo, I am with you always, even unto the end of the world. Amen."

The all-important part, in my opinion, is the spiritual rebirth. Meaning you're spiritually born again. Because how can a man be spiritually reborn if you were never physically born? Basically, you get baptized in the name of the Father, the Son, and the Holy Ghost **because** you're saved, not to GET saved. We trust in Jesus' blood atonement, not getting dunked in plain old water. As a result of our belief and faith in Jesus, we follow his commands as best we can, including baptism!

This admittedly is my likely most shaky interpretation thus far. Let's say my impression is wrong for the sake of argument. Let's look at this as logically as our flesh allows, yes?

Do you think being born again in the spirit is more important, or physically being dunked in your mother's pool outside? I know which answer I'm picking.

Here's Mark 16:16: He that believeth and is baptized shall be saved; but he that **believeth not** shall be damned.

Notice how it didn't say, "but he that believeth not and isn't baptized shall be damned." It says he that believeth not. This shows that belief is paramount for salvation. This means that refusing or omitting baptism is not mentioned as being the cause for damnation, just refusing to believe. If Jesus wanted to ensure we knew baptism was equal to belief, don't you think He would've mentioned it there? Had he done so, the matter would've been settled. Faith saves, as many other Bible verses will testify. Yet, if a believing person is baptized, he is saved—not because baptism saved him but because faith did.

Further verses reinforce this point, like Hebrews 3:19: "So we see that they could not enter in because of unbelief."

John 3:18: "He that believeth on him is not condemned: but he that believeth not is condemned already, because he hath not believed in the name of the only begotten Son of God."

Here's Luke 3:16-17: "John answered, saying unto them all, I indeed baptize you with water; but one mightier than I cometh, the latchet of whose shoes I am not worthy to unloose: he shall baptize you with the Holy Ghost and with fire: Whose fan is in his hand, and he will thoroughly purge his floor, and will gather the wheat into his garner; but the chaff he will burn with fire unquenchable."

I believe the wheat mentioned is us believers and born again saints, while the chaff are those who trust something else for their salvation.

See, when we believe, we're born again. The very nanosecond we believe the gospel, we're spiritually born again, sealed with the Holy Spirit until the day of redemption. That means we're baptized in the Spirit in that moment of belief. That's what's needed for our salvation, I believe.

Remember when I mentioned that once we believe we're free from sin?

Men and women misunderstand this too. They think, "Oh, it must mean I won't sin again, or I'm not really saved."

Is that true, though? No, it means that our spirit cannot sin. Our body? Yeah, it still sins, and remember, the wages of sin is death. Our spirit is free from sin for all time. Our body? Yeah, it's still going to die. After all, it's sinned, God above knows how many times. So yes, part of us is then free from sin — our spirit, that is. Our bodies aren't magically cleansed of our fleshly desires. I sincerely wish it worked that way, but it doesn't.

Moving off Baptism because I believe we've explored enough of it for our purposes, let's return to sinning.

Sin has its punishments beyond death. Let's say I want to go out and fornicate with dozens of women. (Admittedly, most young men think this sounds like a wonderful time, right?) Well, there're consequences to this example, aren't there?

Maybe you get a few pregnant and need to pay child support for eighteen years and ruin yourself financially and complicate their lives exponentially. Perhaps you get those vile STDs that follow you throughout your entire earthly life. Maybe you get entangled with a woman who is, shall we say, clingy and sort of crazy during this. You don't know specifics until they happen, but realize every sin we do has some sort of price we pay.

If you go to rob a convenience store, you go to prison. Maybe someone in that store pulls a gun to end the threat they perceive you as. Maybe their bullet misses and hits someone else. We don't know, so why put you and others in this situation?

If you lie to your neighbor, that could cause all manner of problems, ranging from them merely not trusting your word to real dire consequences. Let's say you lied to them and said their husband's cheating on them, and they kill them! You see?

Do you get my point yet? There are consequences we must face if we sin, whether it be at God's chastening hand, or mortal consequences. The problems sin causes aren't just confined to us. It can alter other people's lives.

Most folks don't want to ruin others' lives because of a sin they commit. Some don't care, but we believers try not to do such things, right? While we try not to sin, inevitably we will until God grants us our glorified bodies, or we die.

Our desire is to try to minimize the impact our sin has on others, yes? Maybe it's just me, but if I sin, I'd rather it only affect me. This is optimistic, granted, but we try.

I'm no saint, and I've likely affected others' lives for the negative. I wasn't always so mindful in my youth. We all learn at different speeds. What matters is that we're trying to minimize our sins. Trying to 'stop' sinning is a fool's errand and can lead you to truly believing that 'I don't sin.'

Remember 1st John 1:8: "If we say that we have no sin, we deceive ourselves, and the truth is not in us."

The best I think we can do is try. We try to stop sinning as best we can. We'll stumble and fall into the proverbial mud along this narrow road we traverse. I stumble on this path every single day, but I get up and keep going. Not by my strength, mind you, but because I lean on God.

Proverbs 24:16: "For a just man falleth seven times, and riseth up again: but the wicked shall fall into mischief."

Bottom line, we should indeed strive to please the Father

by acting to please Him. Will we always succeed? Nope. I wish we could, but until we're made to be sinless by God, we will stumble and fall. What's important is that we lean on God's eternally strong arm to pick us up out of the proverbial muck and keep walking toward that narrow gate (Jesus).

8

8: MOCKERS AND SCOFFERS

This isn't the most fun concept to write about, but I feel I must explain further. Have you ever tried to evangelize to someone, and they laugh in your face, or they crack a joke at your or God's expense? Maybe they deny His power or even His entire existence? It's a somewhat frustrating experience, isn't it? Yes, even a socially withdrawn hermit like me has experienced this before.

We must remember not to allow it to affect us. It shouldn't stop us from trying to spread the gospel far and wide. It's easy for it to discourage us and impede our ministry, but we cannot allow one (hopefully) temporary failure to make us quit. The very next person could believe the gospel instantly. Isn't that worth the risk of temporary embarrassment?

I say this as someone who's very much sensitive. Sure, I sometimes imagine someone who reads my books going, "This guy's clearly nuts," but if you didn't notice, I keep on typing. Why? Because if this book helps one person find Jesus and trust in His blood, I'll be happy as can be.

Now, mockers and scoffers themselves are indeed prophesied in the Bible. Don't believe me? Here's 2nd Peter 3:3-4: "Knowing this first, that there shall come in the last days scoffers, walking after their own lusts, And saying, Where is the promise of his coming? for since the fathers fell asleep, all things continue as they were from the beginning of the creation."

I believe this verse refers to his soon to be rapture and the deniers (and there are many), but let's focus on the rest for now.

Maybe they call you crazy for believing in God; perhaps they say you're delusional for believing in Him. It's tough, but try to remember this verse and realize they're simply fulfilling Bible prophecy. You can try to tell them this, but it'll either bring more mockery or incite anger, I'd imagine. I suppose you can try, but remember what Jesus said in Mathew 7:6: "Give not that which is holy unto the dogs, neither cast ye your pearls before swine, lest they trample them under their feet, and turn again and rend you."

What does that mean? Well, I believe that in Jesus' earthly ministry, dogs weren't the domesticated lovable furballs we know and love nowadays. They were seen more as scavengers and unclean animals. I think this part of his sentence means that some will not respect or appreciate the spiritual truths you lay at their feet.

The pigs part is rather simpler to understand. Swine in Jewish culture are still to this day considered unclean. The concept of throwing pearls - these valuable and precious stones symbolizing wisdom or the knowledge of heaven - I think this means we should exercise wisdom in whom we share the gospel. Some may react with hostility. Still, it's rather impossible to know at a glance who is a proverbial dog or swine. Just know they may not be receptive and accept that reality. In a perfect world, we would share the gospel with everyone! Just understand that there will be those hostile and angry at receiving this wisdom. That's the gist of it, I believe.

For clarity's sake, I'm not saying don't preach the gospel to the lost. They're the very ones who need it most! We should indeed attempt to spread the gospel to them. Just know when to quit and cut your losses. Belaboring the point to someone clearly not interested will only bring more grief to you and possibly danger.

I think the next few sentences of Jesus' words highlight what could happen if we try to force the issue with folks who are clearly not interested. They'll stomp these pearls of wisdom underfoot and, depending on the person, may even attack us!

Still, the most loving act I think you can do is to share the gospel of salvation with the unsaved. Do with that knowledge what you will, but just because someone's hateful at first, your informing them could plant a seed within them. To prove the concept, here's 1st Corinthians 3:6-9: "I have planted, Apollos watered; but God gave the increase. So then neither is he that planteth any thing, neither he that watereth; but God that giveth the increase. Now he that planteth and he that watereth are one: and every man shall receive his own reward according to his own labour. For we are labourers together with God: ye are God's husbandry, ye are God's building." Whether the risk is worth it is up to us.

Here's Proverbs 15:12: "A scorner loveth not one that reproveth him: neither will he go unto the wise."

Other translations change scorner to mocker and a whole host of other things, which is why I stick to the King James version, but that's a whole different book to write about. In this verse, scorners and mockers are rather similar, since mockers typically ridicule or scorn others, showing contempt for wisdom and instruction. The book of Proverbs typically contrasts the wise with the mockers, so that shows us the spectrum we're working with here.

Here's Proverbs 21:24: "Proud and haughty scorner is his name, who dealeth in proud wrath."

Here's another highlighting mockers/scorners. It's in Proverbs 29:8: "Scornful men bring a city into a snare: but wise men turn away wrath."

We seeing a pattern here? Sure, the world considers mocking others to be fashionable. Heck, look at television talk shows, internet influencers, comedians, and movies. Isn't it almost always played for a laugh or comedy or entertainment? I'm not saying we should be humorless and insufferable, but there's a time and place. Wisdom of the Lord and the gospel of salvation is NOT one of these.

Many of these scornful mockers consider themselves right from the get-go. They won't even consider that they could be wrong about eternity. This always strikes me as odd. Aren't you and I wrong about many things every day? Why are they so sure eternity isn't one of those subjects? You got me. Still, that's why we should spread the gospel of salvation. Even if that seed doesn't bloom immediately, it may prove integral later.

What do I mean? Well, I guess this is a more somber note. Many mockers and scoffers who deny the gospel now may well be thrust into the 7-year tribulation soon. When millions of people around the globe disappear in a moment (aka the rapture), they may stop and go, "Oh no, those darn Christians were right?"

See? That's when those seeds could be watered and grow. It's not ideal from where I'm sitting, but some folks only learn the hard way. You know the type? I'm one of them sometimes, so I feel bad for those who retain their hard-hearted ways regarding God, His Son, and the Holy Spirit.

Some of these people say they "Just can't believe." I find this impossible to believe, ironically. Why? As one pastor wiser than I said, "You believe in things every single day of your life. You believe that when you flick a light switch, the light will turn on. Or when you twist your key (or push a button) your car engine will turn on. You're not incapable of believing. It's simply a matter of what you believe."

Some say they can't believe in a God who'll send people to hell. This is easily rebuked with, "What about the God who sent his Son to bleed, suffer, and die for your sin debt?" Or if you prefer, "Jesus loved you so much he'd rather come, bleed, and die on a cross just so he could resurrect and spend eternity with you." These may not work immediately, but that's how I'd answer.

Everyone's capable of belief; it's just what you believe in. Do you believe in human wisdom, or would you rather trust God's? I know who I'd pick.

Mockers and scoffers are not limited to unbelievers either, believe it or not. There are believers who practice this too. You might say, "How?"

Granted, a believer's mocking and scoffing sound entirely different, but the result is rather the same. A believer scoffer might laugh at you for expecting Jesus' return in the clouds soon and say, "You believe in the rapture? Ha, don't you know there's only his second coming? Do you not study?" Whereas an unbeliever would likely blaspheme during their mocking. Both examples aren't exactly fun to be on the receiving end of.

Well, as of the day I type this, the Feast of Trumpets fevered pitch has somewhat calmed down. Guess what sort of videos are being made now.

Yes, that's correct - videos made by believers scoffing at those of us who watch and wait for our glorious Lord's return in the clouds. Why, I've seen video titles like "We survived the 'rapture!'" or other such derisive titles like 'The Pre-Trib Rapture Hoax failed!'. Mind you, this is still on the 24th, so, eh, I imagine the mocking from brothers and sisters will get much worse. Now why?

Well, this parable should explain things better than I ever could. Here's Luke 12:39-46: "And this know, that if the goodman of the house had known what hour the thief would come, he would have watched, and not have suffered his house to be broken through. Be ye therefore ready also: for the Son of man cometh at an hour when ye think not. Then Peter said unto him, Lord, speakest thou this parable unto us, or even to all? And the Lord said, Who then is that faithful and wise steward, whom his lord shall make ruler over his household, to give them their portion of meat in due season? Blessed is that servant, whom his lord when he cometh shall find so doing. Of a truth I say unto you, that he will make him ruler over all that he hath. But and if that servant say in his heart, My lord delayeth his coming; and shall begin to beat the menservants and maidens, and to eat and drink, and to be drunken; The lord of that servant will come in a day when he looketh not for him, and at an hour when he is not aware, and will cut him in sunder, and will appoint him his portion with the unbelievers."

This is clearly talking about those who mock and scoff at the Rapture, in my opinion. Specifically, it's showing the world mocking us. The giveaway that this is referencing the rapture is the thief bit. Even some believers are joining in beating the menservants and maidens. This is not the message of love that Christ preached. Now, if these scoffers are true believers, I don't believe they'll go to hell, but they'll probably get a talking to.

Yes, sometimes our biggest detractors are our own brothers and sisters in Christ! That's difficult to fathom, isn't it? I had a brother growing up. Sure we argued, but when things get tough, I know I can count on him. That's how we should treat each other.

Let me put it this way. If your brother or sister gets excited about an event - let's say, for the sake of example, a concert. Your sibling is so excited their favorite band is coming to your town and is talking about it nonstop. Maybe you have reservations about their arriving that day. Perhaps you've seen some news that's not promising. Then the band reschedules for whatever reason. Are you going to say, "Ha, you idiot, I knew they wouldn't come today! I told you."? No. Hopefully you'd say something like, "I'm sorry, Brother, I know you were looking forward to it, but hopefully they'll come soon."

Perhaps that's not the greatest example, but you get the point. We should show grace to our brothers and sisters, not just regarding the soon to be Rapture, but in all things!

Another example I've seen used recently is two children waiting in their driveway for their father to return. One kid jumps up and bounces in place when he sees a car that looks remotely like their dad's. The other mocks and ridicules his brother, saying, "You fool, I told you that wasn't him. He's not coming back yet." Which would you be happier to see when you return home if you were the dad?

One last example. Picture you're married. You return home and open the front door. Do you want your spouse to be waiting to deliver a hug and kiss when you get home? Or would you rather open the door and announce your presence and all you receive is "Ok."

These all illustrate why I imagine the Lord instructed us to watch for his return. Heck, one verse even poses a question that's interesting. Luke 18:8: "I tell you that he will avenge them speedily. Nevertheless when the Son of man cometh, shall he find faith on the earth?"

We know the answer for the world at large. The unbelieving world won't have faith, but us? We should have faith in his return! Why argue and squabble while pointing fingers?

We should be careful that we're not found sitting in the seat of mockers. Here's Psalm 1:1: "Blessed is the man that walketh not in the counsel of the ungodly, nor standeth in the way of sinners, nor sitteth in the seat of the scornful."

Even if you're saved, I imagine we could have some uncomfortable conversations if we're found sitting in the seat of mockers and scoffers. Imagine being asked by the Lord himself. "Why did you discourage your brothers and sisters regarding my return? Do you know how many people's crowns you stole? They loved my return until your scoffing and mocking."

That is not a question I'd want to answer - just saying.

That's why I'm here trying to encourage every one of you. I know this is a long passage of scripture, but boy, these words are more relevant today than they've ever been in the body of Christ. Here's 1st Thessalonians 5: 1-22: "But of the times and the seasons, brethren, ye have no need that I write unto you. For yourselves know perfectly that the day of the Lord so cometh as a thief in the night. For when they shall say, Peace and safety; then sudden destruction cometh upon them, as travail upon a woman with child; and they shall not escape. But ye, brethren, are not in darkness, that that day should overtake you as a thief. Ye are all the children of light, and the children of the day: we are not of the night, nor of darkness. Therefore let us not sleep, as do others; but let us watch and be sober. For they that sleep sleep in the night; and they that be drunken are drunken in the night. But let us, who are of the day, be sober, putting on the breastplate of faith and love; and for an helmet, the hope of salvation. For God hath not appointed us to wrath, but to obtain salvation by our Lord Jesus Christ, Who died for us, that, whether we wake or sleep, we should live together with him. Wherefore comfort yourselves together, and edify one another, even as also ye do. And we beseech you, brethren, to know them which labor among you, and are over you in the Lord, and admonish you; And to esteem them very highly in love for their work's sake. And be at peace among yourselves. Now we exhort you, brethren, warn them that are unruly, comfort the feebleminded, support the weak, be patient toward all men. See that none render evil for evil unto any man; but ever follow that which is good, both among yourselves, and to all men. Rejoice evermore. Pray without ceasing. In every thing give thanks: for this is the will of God in Christ Jesus concerning you. Quench not the Spirit. Despise not prophesyings. Prove all things; hold fast that which is good. Abstain from all appearance of evil."

That was surely a mouthful. That passage is obviously referring to the Rapture. You know, that thing some deny wholeheartedly is even in the Bible. It also tells us how to treat each other. It orders us to warn the unruly, edify (build each other up), recognize and respect our elders, and to learn from them. That passage also mentions that we comfort the feebleminded, support the weak, and be patient towards all men. We shouldn't despise prophecy off the rip but test it and hold fast to that which is good. (Meaning, don't call folks false prophets before those dates come to pass.) Now, if those dates pass and their prophecy doesn't pass, call them out, but be careful. If God does send prophecy through someone, you don't want to call Him a liar accidentally before those dates pass! It seems so very simple, doesn't it? You'd be surprised how little grace that's going around on the internet and in person nowadays. It's a sad state of affairs, this world.

Thankfully, there's nothing saying we must be chronically online. I know I should learn that lesson myself, but studying, reading, and trying to read our Bibles more would be wise. I don't pray nearly enough, so I have things to work on. How about you?

9

9: DOING WHAT WE CAN

If you've read my previous book "My Visit to Heaven," then you understand that believers from all walks of life are struggling with serving our Lord. You know that I'm a modern-day hermit, and I only leave my home to go to church, the dentist, etc. I rarely have the opportunity to share the gospel of salvation with someone because of my social anxiety. How would I go about doing it?

Well, you're reading it. The Lord gave me the talent of writing, and I'm trying to use it for His glory and to lead more to Him and His Son. This is the only possible way I can preach since I have stage fright, social anxiety, and a whole host of issues.

Maybe you're not as socially withdrawn - great! Maybe you can share the gospel in the store next time you meet an old friend from high school. Perhaps volunteering at Church is within your power. You can teach your children, nieces, nephews, grandchildren about Jesus, etc. Think about what you can do. I bet there are some avenues you hadn't considered. Remember, we'll be rewarded according to our labor, so let's build up some treasures for ourselves in heaven.

Mind you, I believe those rewards are probably crowns. Those crowns we'll toss at Jesus' feet. Don't you want to have something to give to our savior? I sure do!

I know you do too, so don't delay like I did. A quick recap for those who didn't read my previous book: I was a prodigal son for over eighteen years. I was saved at age 12 or 13 and became prodigal at age 18. Being prodigal sounds fun on the surface to our mortal reasoning, but I can assure you, it's not.

I wasted almost twenty years that I could've been trying to serve our Lord, and instead I was following my own desires. I'm ashamed of those years, if I'm honest. Were they fun? For a season, but eventually those years morphed into ages of anger, despair, loneliness, drug abuse, and corruption. If I'd been writing during those years instead, who knows if I'd have become like I am today. Maybe I wouldn't have social anxiety. Perhaps I'd have written far more books to preach the blood. Who knows?

How about you? Are you wasting time? I'm not judging you, because I was on that road for nearly two decades! It's such an easy road to take from our mortal perspectives, isn't it? After all, who doesn't want to go out and do what they want?

Well, nobody said the life of a believer was meant to be easy. We're supposed to deny our own lusts of the flesh, but man, we both understand how difficult that is, don't we? It goes against every fiber of our being to deny ourselves and walk in the Spirit.

Yet that's what we're called to do. Talk about a tall order, am I right?

So what are we waiting for? Let's figure out the best way

we can serve. Maybe you're in a similar or worse situation than I am. Then pray from home! You can always be what they call a "prayer warrior". Folks everywhere need intercessory prayers, trust me. You might never tell them you're praying for them, and you'll still be helping them.

If I can preach his blood in book form, imagine what you can accomplish. I'm nothing but a guy who stays at home, writes, plays video games, and helps my elderly parents around the house. Who are you, and what can you do?

I'm not saying turn your life upside down to do outlandish things. Even printing out "salvation cards" and handing them out could help. Maybe you have an unsaved friend who's going through depression, and you could share the good news? I don't know your life, and frankly, I don't need to. Every man and woman knows their life far better than some random brother in Christ online will ever know.

I've heard tales of folks printing salvation cards out and handing them out at various places. I've never printed off salvation cards, but I imagine they're like little business cards that have the bloodstained gospel on it. Handing them out could guide someone's soul to Jesus. Even if handing out cards isn't your thing, you can find your own calling. I'm simply giving examples and throwing out ideas.

If all else fails, pray and ask. I think many underestimate just how much of a blessing it is that we can boldly come before the throne of God and talk to him directly. Here's Hebrews 4:16: "Let us therefore come boldly unto the throne of grace, that we may obtain mercy, and find grace to help in time of need."

Here's the verse showing when we could approach His throne. It's Matthew 27:51-54: "And, behold, the veil of the temple was rent in twain from the top to the bottom; and the earth did quake, and the rocks rent; And the graves were opened; and many bodies of the saints which slept arose, And came out of the graves after his resurrection, and went into the holy city, and appeared unto many. Now when the centurion, and they that were with him, watching Jesus, saw the earthquake, and those things that were done, they feared greatly, saying, Truly this was the Son of God."

When that veil tore asunder, separating the holiest of holies from the congregation, it showed that we didn't need a high priest to talk to God directly. What a blessing that is! I'm guilty of not praying enough.

Here's the tricky part, at least for me. Hearing God's answer is hard. If you pray and ask what you can do, I have no advice for deciphering his answer. It's one of my weaknesses as a believer. I've only "felt" the Lord putting something on my heart a handful of times, and it's obvious what he wanted to communicate. Normally? Yeah, no. I'm deaf as a rock because I never can quite tell what he says.

Here's the best I've got. If you pray and ask a question, you likely won't hear an audible answer. I wish we could hear His voice, but that'd be too easy, I suppose. If you suddenly have an idea pop into your head that relates to that question, it might well be His answer. I'd recommend talking to an elder believer you know and discuss it with them. They'd probably have more insight than I do regarding hearing God's answers.

Regardless, let's not dawdle and twiddle our thumbs. I'm of the belief that Jesus' return will be soon! We're running out of time down here, judging by the geopolitical developments we see every single day. How much proverbial road do we really think this world has left? It's not much, folks.

I'm not trying to scare you, but world leaders are throwing around the threat of nuclear war like rice at a wedding. Used to be, you'd never hear someone threatening with nukes. Now? It's almost an everyday affair. One of these days, someone will push that little red button, and many people will die, sadly.

It's baffling to non-believers just how nonchalant we feel about these things. Don't let these things trouble you if you belong to the King of Kings and the Lord of Lords. Worst case is we die.

Here's 2nd Corinthians 5: 6-8: "Therefore we are always confident, knowing that, whilst we are at home in the body, we are absent from the Lord: (For we walk by faith, not by sight:) We are confident, I say, and willing rather to be absent from the body, and to be present with the Lord."

Meaning if we die, we're with God anyway, so why worry? We have no reason to be afraid. Now, I don't wish to die; don't get me wrong. I trust in God's plan, and it's infallible. He's not rattled or worried, so why should we be?

Some believe that when the nukes fall, we go up (rapture). I don't know the timing, the date, or specifics. What I know is this world can't go on like this for much longer, so let's do the most we can with our remaining time down here.

10

10: DAILY GOALS AS WE WAIT

This isn't a section where I tell you what to do since I'm still learning while traversing the same narrow path as you. Maybe it's me telling myself my shortcomings, and you can learn from it? I'm not sure. This might end up in a rant, but here we go.

I need to pray more every single day. Sure, I like to pray when I first awake and before I try to sleep, along with any time I think of it. I suppose I should endeavor to pray more, and it would help me battle the lusts of the flesh, like it says in Galatians 5:16: "This I say then, Walk in the Spirit, and ye shall not fulfil the lust of the flesh."

That's not especially easy for me to do. Often I go long stretches in the day without saying a word to the Lord. I almost have to manually remind myself to do so. In a perfect world, I'd always be praying like it says in 1st Thessalonians 5:15-18: "See that none render evil for evil unto any man; but ever follow that which is good, both among yourselves, and to all men. Rejoice evermore. Pray without ceasing. In every thing give thanks: for this is the will of God in Christ Jesus concerning you."

How do I fix it? I don't know. I've resorted to reminding myself when it's been a while.

Besides prayer, I surely don't spread the gospel enough in my everyday life. My books are the only place where I really share the good news. Sure, some may say that's enough. How many people write books for the Lord? A lot actually, and the odds that a non-believer will download mine and trust in Christ's blood? It's a slight chance, but I trust the Lord in this matter, like always. It's all I can do. I don't talk to various people throughout the day like most people. I'm cooped up here by my personal choices, so I have nobody to blame but myself.

Sound familiar? We all make poor decisions that we stand behind for whatever reason. Mine are simply especially dumb when I type them out and want to laugh at myself.

I sometimes find myself bored, and instead of watching a sermon online, I'll watch something considerably more worldly. Deep down, I know I shouldn't, but I do anyway. Sometimes you just want to be entertained and laugh, but that's not exactly walking in the spirit, is it?

I'm like you, a version that stays at home whenever given the chance and does things I know I shouldn't occasionally. If you asked me why, I can't give an intelligent answer other than, "A deep part of me really wanted to!"

That's not a good reason, is it? Yeah, I know. I suppose you could consider that idolatry, huh? I'm prioritizing what I want rather than what God wants me to do.

Ever heard of the phrase "wrestling with God"? Boy, I do that every day. God knows my every move and still engages in this proverbial song and dance with me because of his love and patience. What a loving God we have, folks. No, I've never 'won' that wrestling match, yet I still engage in it.

If your kids did something similar, how many days would it take before you lost your temper? Maybe they don't want to do a particular chore, so they duck out and verbally wrestle with you about performing it. If it were me, I'd maybe last four days before I lost my temper and chastened them.

I should yield more to the Lord's will, but I'll be honest, it's tough. Every fiber of our being wants what's entertaining. It doesn't want to read the Bible. I used to tell myself. "Oh, but reading the Bible's boring."

Does that make it better? No, of course not. Besides, when you really dig in and study the Bible, it gets more and more interesting. That's why I sometimes read God's word multiple times a day.

While I may only have a scheduled reading immediately following waking up, I'll often read throughout my day and won't have a reason. This is good, I figure. At least that's one positive habit I've been forming. There aren't many I have if I'm honest.

I'd love to tell you I have it all figured out, but I don't. Ever heard a pastor tell you they don't sin often, and they sort of brag about it? Yeah, I have too. No, I don't believe them when they say it, regardless of who they are. We're all mortal until God changes us. Then I'll believe someone who says they don't sin, because we won't be able to. All the holier than thou preaching people do nowadays, do they think it makes people want to believe? Usually this is accompanied by accusations online by these types too. Accusations that stoke fear, hurt, and nastiness aren't the way to go about evangelizing.

Ever seen those people on sidewalks with those colorful signs that say, "Turn or burn!"? I have. Fear of God is good, yes. Trying to instill fear of God into non-believers is just going to rub them the wrong way. It comes across as "Believe what I believe, or you're burning in hell!" That's technically correct (Assuming they trust Jesus's blood for their salvation, not their 'turning from sin.') Do you seriously think random folks on the street corner like getting barked at and basically threatened with hellfire while they're trying to commute to work?

It doesn't help. All it does is drive unbelievers away who think they have to be perfect or go to hell. They figure, "Why try? I can't be perfect, so I'll keep going my way and at least I'll have fun."

You get my point? I've watched condescending folks tell preachers who tout the blood of Jesus as the way to heaven that they're "misleading their congregation and tickling their ears." Or that they're disobedient and a heretic for preaching the blood. Boy, how some people are lost while totally confident that they're correct. I guess they ignore the part where "turning from sins" is quite prideful. One to think you CAN turn from all sins, and two for always looking down on us who can't. Let's, for the sake of argument, say you could turn from all sins (you can't). What about all those sins before you started? You need remittance for those sins too, you know. So, that entire line of thinking just falls apart. I suppose they think Christ's sacrifice only covers past sins? If so, they need to learn the totality of what Jesus willingly did for us.

Why are so many nasty towards those of us who rely on God's grace? Because we don't preach that you 'turn from sin' to be saved? Is it because we're relying on the Lord's mercy instead of our own works? Okay then. I'll trust the Lord's word; you can trust the man who told you that turning from sin saves you. I'd recommend you don't, but we Bible believers will be sad knowing where you might end up. Please stop trusting in yourselves, people. Haven't we all proved that we're wicked in this corruptible mortal body? How many times a day do you sin?

Me? I've no clue. Probably too many to count. Do I try to stop? Absolutely, but I fail.

I'm repeating myself from chapters ago, but I can't help it. Online, it's rare to find anyone with the real gospel anymore. It's all modernized if you haven't noticed. Blood's icky and barbaric, so they remove it. Gotta keep the pews filled so the offering plate stays full!

I'm generalizing. Not all churches do this, but a lot nowadays surely do. You'll know them when you see them. They seem more like a show you go to every week. These types of churches are more worldly than ever. Heck, I saw an especially egregious example of this recently. Said church had super bowl team banners hanging, and the so-called pastor and company kicked the Bible to mock kick a field goal for heaven's sake! Sometimes they sound more like a political ramble; other times they're like a comedy show, but rarely do they ever speak about what's inside the word of God anymore.

Sure, they may give you their interpretation of the word of God, but rarely do they actually, you know, read the verses word for word. That's quite important, because shocker, even if you're a pastor, you're not infallible.

That's why I try to back up my lessons with specific verses to show I didn't just make it up. Maybe I'm wrong sometimes, maybe not. At least the verses are there so you can pray and ask the Holy Spirit for guidance and ask if I'm completely off base. Perhaps I'm wrong, and I'd rather you make your own decisions on scripture. Most pastors in these mega churches, you're lucky if they even reference scripture, never mind read it!

Sorry for my rant there. It's certainly not your fault. The whole point of this section is this. Nowadays it's more important than ever to stay inside the word of God and read it for yourself. Don't just listen to some guy or woman on the internet and call it a day. Compare what they say to the Bible and see if it's correct or not before believing it instantly. This includes me too. Check my work; I'm certainly not perfect!

If I'd skipped this step, I'd still believe I have to 'turn from sin' to stay saved. Imagine my surprise when I read this from Colossians 2:2: "That their hearts might be comforted, being knit together in love, and unto all riches of the full assurance of understanding, to the acknowledgement of the mystery of God, and of the Father, and of Christ."

That's a little complicated, but it basically means that once you know of Christ's redemptive work, trust him for your salvation, you KNOW you're saved. You have assurance, and that helps to fight off those doubts that spring up from time to time. The mystery it speaks of, for those curious, I think, is about God's redemptive plans for humanity. (aka Jesus dying and bleeding on that cross on Calvary.)

At least, that's my understanding. I'm positive someone out there disagrees with me.

11

11: CLOSING THOUGHTS

Alright, thanks for sticking with me through this entire book. This book is the proverbial "milk" for newfound believers and not "meat" You don't give a newborn babe meat, right? It is the same with being born again. You need the basics before you dive into the complicated concepts.

Let's all try to form better habits regarding the Lord, including me. I have certainly not fully arrived yet or have all the answers. I hope this book has encouraged you and edified you. Encouragement is rare nowadays.

It's all fear-mongering for clicks, which turn into cash online. You know the videos I'm talking about. "Ten signs you're actually going to hell!" type titles for videos. "Signs you're a fake Christian" types.

To be clear, those who make those probably think they're doing a service and helping those they view as deceived. The problem is they're not really in any position to teach. Teaching God's word is a heavy task. I do not make this book lightly since I worry about leading anyone astray. I fear many nowadays do not share this concern and, in their zeal to spread the Lord's word, may misunderstand passages and doctrine.

Note, I'm not saying I'm flawless, just that I respect that teaching God's word is a solemn duty not to be taken lightly. This passage highlights it perfectly. This is from James 3:1: "My brethren, be not many masters, knowing that we shall receive the greater condemnation."

It basically means don't rush to teach others because teachers will be held to a higher standard. If your teachings lead a man toward that broad road of Hell, well, it won't be a fun conversation with the Lord, I imagine.

That's why I pray before every writing session that the Lord guides my hands and delivers the words he wants read here. If anything's messed up, it's clearly my imperfection that screwed it up. I honestly never wanted to teach anything in my life. Too many ignore the dangers of teaching.

They never consider, "What if what I'm teaching is wrong?". Teach a kid wrong in primary school, they're ill-equipped for middle school. Teach an unbelieving man wrong regarding salvation, and you're leading him onto the path to Hell! That's not a responsibility we should ignore, folks.

All too often nowadays, everyone's in a hurry to teach others. Maybe it's for clicks, clout, a genuine desire to help, or whatever the reason. Unless you are 100% sure about salvation, I wouldn't touch that with a twenty-foot pole. That should tell you how certain I am about Jesus' perfect and atoning blood he spilled on our account.

I'm not a bold man, if you hadn't gathered. I'm timid, shy, and uncertain about many things. Salvation isn't one of them because I stand on the word of God. When in doubt, take a stand on God's promises, because he doesn't lie.

Remember the gospel when in doubt, folks. 1st Corinthians 15:1-4. “Moreover, brethren, I declare unto you the gospel which I preached unto you, which also ye have received, and wherein ye stand. By which also ye are saved, if ye keep in memory what I preached unto you, unless ye have believed in vain. For I delivered unto you first of all that which I also received, how that Christ died for our sins according to the scriptures; And that he was buried, and that he rose again the third day according to the scriptures:”

You stand on God’s promises, and you build your eternal house on unshakeable rock, not on shifting sand. Don’t let yourself be flung about by every wind of doctrine like Ephesians 4:14 says: “That we henceforth be no more children, tossed to and fro, and carried about with every wind of doctrine, by the sleight of men, and cunning craftiness, whereby they lie in wait to deceive.”

If you’re not sure about something, pray and ask, or study your Bible and hear it from His Word. Don’t rely on pastors or scholars or whatever else. We trust God above all, not manmade traditions.

Remember, this world is not our home. We’re merely travelers passing through. Don’t let this world’s traditions, philosophies, and other things influence you too much. We stand firm on God’s promises, not men’s best guesses about God.

Which is to say, I think we’re all supposed to study God’s Word ourselves, but I’m guilty of this myself. For over 36 years, I never studied my Bible. Only just recently did I start, and this book is a compilation of all I’ve learned, meagre as it is.

I don’t know what else to say, so I’ll leave you with this.

When you’re down, depressed, struggling, and wondering how you’ll make it to tomorrow, remember that

God's always there with you, dear brother/sister. He never leaves you, forsakes you, or leaves you alone in that valley. God accompanies you and gives you the strength you need. No, it won't be fun, but iron sharpens iron, meaning tough times strengthen you. Ultimately, I think God wants his children to grow up big and strong like we want our children to, right?

He doesn't enjoy watching us suffer, same as we don't enjoy seeing our kids going through a rough time. Just remember, he never abandons his children. Here's Isiah 41:10: Fear thou not; for I am with thee: be not dismayed; for I am thy God: I will strengthen thee; yea, I will help thee; yea, I will uphold thee with the right hand of my righteousness.

Above all, here's what helps and still astonishes me to this day. Once you believe in Jesus' blood atonement for your salvation, God sees you as righteous and not a sinner anymore. Isn't that mind blowing? Here's Hebrews 11:7: "By faith Noah, being warned of God of things not seen as yet, moved with fear, prepared an ark to the saving of his house; by the which he condemned the world, and became heir of the righteousness which is by faith."

Or a more plain verse if you prefer in Isaiah 43:25: "I, even I, am he that blotteth out thy transgressions for mine own sake, and will not remember thy sins."

How about another? Here's Jeremiah 31:34: "And they shall teach no more every man his neighbor, and every man his brother, saying, Know the LORD: for they shall all know me, from the least of them unto the greatest of them, saith the LORD: for I will forgive their iniquity, and I will remember their sin no more."

So, as you see, once you're saved, God forgets your sins for his own reasons. I imagine it's because of the boundless love he has for his children because he's the perfect Father. That's an encouraging thought, isn't it?

During our worst days, he still sees us as righteous and eagerly awaits our return home. That fills me with warm hope just typing those words.

We worship a God who is capable of love, wrath, jealously, kindness, and all manner of emotions, and he loves his children with a fierceness I cannot even describe.

With that, remember, folks, it's not about perfection; it's about where we're going. Whether we draw our last breath or Jesus descends into the clouds and escorts us home, this Earth is not our home. Our possessions down here are temporary, and it's best we try to remember that. Home is where the heart is, and that means heaven awaits us...

THANK YOU FOR READING!

I pray this book helped you in your search for salvation and blessed you. I hope you have a blessed day! If you'd like to support this work, please consider leaving an honest review on Amazon. Have a great day.

ABOUT THE AUTHOR

Alexander J Fischer has written two spiritual books and aims to possibly write more, should the Holy Spirit guide him.

He writes action/adventure books under the alternate pen name of Alex J. Fischer. (Reader discretion advised, they contain strong language, violence, adult themes, etc.)

ALSO BY ALEXANDER J FISCHER

My recounting of my Near Death Experience:

My Visit to Heaven

You can find my fiction books here: (Be warned, they have adult themes, intense violence, and strong language.)

https://www.amazon.com/stores/author/B09K5NHVGX?i

www.ingramcontent.com/pod-product-compliance
Lightning Source LLC
LaVergne TN
LVHW011048110826
845149LV00015B/3400

* 9 7 8 1 9 5 6 2 8 1 4 8 4 *